JAZZ

AN AMERICAN SAGA

JAMES LINCOLN COLLIER

HENRY HOLT AND COMPANY | NEW YORK

Henry Holt and Company, LLC
Publishers since 1866
115 West 18th Street
New York, New York 10011

Henry Holt is a registered
trademark of Henry Holt and Company, LLC

Published in Canada by Fitzhenry & Whiteside Ltd.,
195 Allstate Parkway, Markham, Ontario L3R 4T8.

Library of Congress Cataloging-in-Publication Data
Collier, James Lincoln.
Jazz : an American saga / James Lincoln Collier.
p.   cm.
Includes bibliographical references and index.
Summary: Examines the origins of jazz, its variety,
greatness, and individual artists.
1. Jazz—History and criticism—Juvenile literature.   [1. Jazz—
History and criticism.]   I. Title.
ML3508.C   781.65'09—dc21   97-3004

ISBN 0-8050-4121-4

First Edition—1997

Printed in the United States of America
on acid-free paper. ∞

3 5 7 9 10 8 6 4 2

Book design by Debbie Glasserman

All photographs appearing in this book, unless
otherwise noted, are supplied by the author.

FOR THE GOGAN CHILDREN

CONTENTS

JAZZ
AN AMERICAN SAGA

CHAPTER 1

THE AMERICAN SPIRIT
OF JAZZ

Sometime around 1900, out in the Louisiana countryside to the west of the city of New Orleans, a little group of teenagers sit on wood boxes and barrels in a musty old barn. They are dark-skinned—some lighter, some darker—a blend of black and white races so common in the New Orleans area. Sunlight falls through the open door of the barn, making a yellow square on the dirt floor, and more sunlight streams in shafts through knotholes and cracks in the barn walls.

These teenagers are playing musical instruments. One has a guitar, another a battered cornet, another a wooden snare drum with patched heads and varnish peeling from the sides, another a metal clarinet, another a tarnished trombone. They have had little training in music, except what they have worked out for themselves, along with a few tips from older musicians in the little farm town they live in.

But they are not really much interested in the kind of music the older musicians play—the marches, church hymns, and old favorites like "De Camptown Races" and "Old Folks at Home," which they break out for Sunday concerts in the town square, or dances in the Grange Hall on Saturday nights.

True, the music these teenagers are playing is not entirely different from that of their uncles, fathers, and older brothers. They play many of the same tunes—hymns like "Just a Closer Walk with Thee," and popular songs like "Won't You Come Home, Bill Bailey?" But there is something different about these tunes when the teenagers play them. There is a lilt to them, a jumpiness that is absent from the older music.

These teenagers sitting on boxes and barrels in that sunlit barn could not really tell you what it is that is different about their music, nor where they got the idea for it. Somehow, it had just been there, hanging in the air, waiting for someone to reach out for it. These are, we must remember, kids without much musical training. They are going more by feel than by knowledge. Their music is rough, sometimes out of tune. They miss a lot of notes, get a lot of them wrong. But they are not troubled by their mistakes, for what matters to them is getting that lilt, that swing into the music. And so they play through the long, hot afternoon, until the shadows begin to grow long and some adult comes out of the cabin and barks at them to quit, the music is driving the grown-ups crazy.

This music, would, in time, drive a lot of other people crazy as it drifted out of New Orleans, spread from there across the United States, and then around the world. But for every person who disliked it, there would be another one who got from it an infectious feeling that made you want to tap your foot, swing your hips, and start to dance.

Is this how jazz started? The truth is that we do not really know for sure, and we probably never will know. There were no tape recorders in those days, no records or CDs. That music vanished into the air of sunny afternoons and hot southern nights. Fortunately, forty and fifty years ago a few jazz scholars sought out some of the people who had

One of the very earliest jazz bands was this one led by trombonist Edward "Kid" Ory (second from left). The other musicians are Edward Robinson, drums; Chif Matthews, trumpet; Raymond Brown, violin; Stonewall Matthews, guitar; Harry Foster, string bass. This group of teenagers played a type of music that developed into jazz—they helped to invent the music form. Violins were standard in early jazz bands and usually doubled the melody with the trumpet.

been around at the time—some of those very teenagers in that barn grown old—and talked to them about how the music was in the old days. These interviews help to give us some idea of how and when jazz sprung into being. Although we see the details only vaguely, as through a mist, the description I have given of it is probably as good a guess as any.

One thing we can be sure of is that jazz was invented in America. Only in the United States was there precisely the right combination of black and white cultures for its creation. And America remains its home, the place where jazz is most tightly mixed into the life of its citizens, despite its popularity in many other countries. It today grips young people who might have been the great-grandchildren of those pioneers playing in that sunlit barn.

Over this long century American life has changed radically: where those Louisiana teenagers hardly ever traveled beyond the limits of their own town, and traveled mostly by foot or horse cart when they went anywhere, we think nothing of jumping on a plane and flying across a continent in an afternoon; where those teenagers never saw a movie, never heard recorded sound of any kind, never listened to a radio program, we spend half our waking hours engaged one way or another with canned entertainment; where those kids, and millions of Americans like them, lived in homes without electricity and running water, read at night by oil lamp and bathed in water drawn from a pump and heated on a woodstove, we have refrigerators that pour out ice cubes with the press of a button, devices that can turn machines on and off by phone from a thousand miles away. In the midst of this, jazz

Jazz first attracted the interest of Europeans in the late 1920s, and by the end of World War II it was an international phenomenon. Here is Benny Goodman shaking hands with Premier Nikita Khrushchev of Russia during a tour there in 1962.

Jazz has been played everywhere in America, from the roughest nightclubs to Carnegie Hall. At left, Pete Lala's club, where Louis Armstrong and many other pioneering jazz musicians played during the heyday of jazz in New Orleans. This picture was taken many years later. At right, Benny Goodman rehearsing with Leonard Bernstein, composer and conductor of the New York Philharmonic.

continues to live as the world changes around it, seeing fads and fashions in clothing and art come and go. It has shown a lasting power. Clearly, there is some very basic appeal to a music that can attract a country teenager in 1905, a Russian taxi driver in 1935, a Japanese professor in 1965, and a Bangkok vegetable seller in 1997.

Still, nowhere else is jazz so threaded through life as it is in America. Today jazz is taught in most colleges and universities. Many high schools have their jazz ensembles, and you can even find jazz groups in junior high schools. Nothing like this system of jazz education exists outside of America.

You can always find jazz being played in many, if not most, major cities around the world, including some improbable ones. There is plenty of jazz in Tokyo, Moscow, Prague, São Paulo, and Melbourne. But in other countries, once you get away from the capital cities, it is hard to find live jazz. The opposite is true in the United States. Jazz is played regularly in our small cities, like Danbury, Connecticut, Billings, Montana, and Columbia, South Carolina. Indeed, jazz turns

More than any other musician, Louis Armstrong personifies jazz. His great solos with the Hot Five in the 1920s showed the world that jazz was more than just a music to dance to, but could be considered an art. By the end of his life he was the best-known jazz musician in the world. This picture shows him as he was rising in popularity during the 1930s. *Courtesy of the Institute of Jazz Studies, Rutgers University.*

up in even smaller places: you can frequently hear jazz in little towns like Cold Spring, New York, where there is a band shell in a small park overlooking the Hudson River, or in La Crosse, Wisconsin, where there is an annual jazz fest.

Jazz is woven into the fabric of our culture in a way that it is not elsewhere. We are not surprised to find a jazz band at a wedding, at a political rally, at a tailgate party in a parking lot before a football game, at the opening of a new store in a mall, even at a reception at the White House. Not all Americans like jazz, by any means, any more than all Americans are interested in baseball, or fishing. But jazz is something we are used to, something we are as familiar with as baseball and fishing. To one degree or another, it touches all of our lives.

What was it about the United States that made it so much more receptive to jazz than any other nation, as is still the case? It is because we Americans as a people are unique in certain ways. For one, America is a land of newcomers. True, some of us, like those kids in that sunlit barn banging away at their music on battered instruments, come from families that have been in the country for many generations. Others of us have grandparents, or even parents, who were born in other lands. Many of us came to the United States ourselves as children. We are a people who accept change, indeed seek out new ways of doing things, of seeing the world. Of course we have our traditions, our habits, our folkways, like shooting off fireworks on the Fourth of July and eating turkey on Thanksgiving. But we are a restless people, always on the lookout for something new. We like novelty, and we are quick to accept the newest style in clothes, the hot young movie star. When jazz came along at the beginning of the twentieth century, it struck Americans of that time as the exciting new thing.

And we Americans have always been strongly individualistic, more so than people in many other places. We admire people who do not always go along with the gang. We think it is a good thing to "march

The English were among the first non-Americans to become interested in jazz. Both Duke Ellington and Louis Armstrong made tours there in the early 1930s. Here Ellington talks with Princess Margaret. *Courtesy of RCA Records.*

to a different drummer." This individualism is not always to the good, for at times it slips into mere selfishness, putting our own interests ahead of those of everyone else. Nonetheless, for good or ill, we are an individualistic people. It is not surprising, therefore, that we have so taken to the idea of the individual jazz soloist standing up in front of the band and "telling his story," as jazz musicians sometimes say. To be sure, the big swing band—with twelve to fifteen musicians working as a closely coordinated team—has always been part of jazz. But at the heart of the music is the soloist going it alone. Our greatest heroes are not the composers and arrangers of big band music, but a Louis Armstrong or a Charlie Parker stepping out front to invent on the spot a blazing-hot, hard-swinging solo.

This American interest in novelty and admiration for individualism add up to another aspect of the American spirit. That is the knack for inventiveness. We are always looking for solutions to problems, better ways of doing things. Some of our biggest national celebrities are inventors like Thomas Edison, who played a large role in creating the movies, the phonograph, the electric light. Once again, this is not always completely to the good, for often we junk old ways just because they are old, without considering the value in them. Nonetheless, one of the great appeals jazz has for us is that the music is constantly being invented—improvised at the moment. Somebody is always coming up with a new style, a new way of playing the music. It is ceaselessly churning, and the jazz musicians we most admire are those who, like Armstrong, Parker, Dizzy Gillespie, John Coltrane, come up with new styles.

Jazz has, of course, been taken up in many other places around the world. The music was becoming an international phenomenon as long ago as the early 1930s, when the first great non-American jazz musician, Django Reinhardt, began to play with the Quintet of the Hot Club of France. A Gypsy, Django could not read or write, much less read music, but he had an astonishing instinct for music and showed that others besides Americans could swing.

CHAPTER 2

THE CRADLE OF JAZZ

There is no doubt at all that jazz first burst out in New Orleans and the countryside around that city. There simply are no reports of it appearing anywhere else until it was already well known in that area.

What was it about New Orleans that made it the cradle of jazz? To understand jazz, we have to know something about the people who created it. We begin, therefore, with the people of Africa, especially West Africa, where the bulk of the slaves brought to the Americas came from. To these people, music was very important, almost as important as speech. It was woven through their daily lives. They sang work songs as they pounded corn into flour or tugged at heavy fish nets, to ease the monotony of their labor. They had music to accompany virtually every important event in their lives, down to the appearance of the first tooth in a child's mouth. They sometimes sang arguments in court or to praise a king. The best known of their music, however, was the rich and complex kind produced by master musicians to accompany major religious and social ceremonies—a marriage, a funeral, the preparation for a hunt or warfare.

A Lakas tribal orchestra from West Africa. The men on the left are playing bailophones, or xylophones. Gourds are hung from each of the bars as resonators to make the sound louder.

The music produced at these ceremonies involved everybody in the community, not just the musicians. The people were not there as an audience, but to actively participate by dancing, clapping their hands, or singing responses to lines from the band. These ceremonies—with their drums of different sizes, their gongs, rattles and scrapers, the dancers stomping on the earth and twirling in circles, the hand clapping and singing—were rich and impressive.

This West African tribal music is far too complex for me to describe in detail here. Suffice it to say that at its heart was a complicated system of overlapping rhythms, usually made by drums but often sung or played by flutes, bells, scrapers, and other kinds of instruments. Sometimes as many as six different rhythms, or "beats," rode along side by side, meshing and unmeshing as they went. This music was rhythmically far more complex than European music. Try beating two beats with one hand and three beats with the other at the same time. Musicians learn to do this, and so can you, given practice. Then imagine how much training it must have taken for African musicians to learn to beat five beats against six.

When the Africans were brought to the New World as slaves, the memory of this music came with them—indeed, some of the slaves were master musicians. Frequently the slavers made them bring their drums and other instruments, and forced the slaves in chains to come up on the deck of the slave ship to sing and dance, the idea being that they would be happier and healthier if they were allowed such recreation.

The same idea held after the slaves reached the Americas: they were encouraged to sing as they worked, on the theory that they would be more cheerful and less rebellious if they had their music. Thus, African music was kept alive in the Americas for well over a hundred years, as new slaves arrived into the nineteenth century.

But at the same time the slaves were picking up European music. When we think of the slave South we usually envision a huge white mansion surrounded by vast fields where gangs of blacks are picking cotton or hoeing tobacco while a whip-bearing overseer on horseback looks on. Certainly such places existed. But the majority of black slaves lived on small farms, usually owned by a single white family. A small farmer might have only a few slaves, perhaps only one or two. Often it would be a black family of a father, a mother, and a couple of children. The white family on such a farm usually worked alongside their slaves. They often prayed together, ate much the same food, wore much the same clothing—blacks often were given the patched and faded hand-me-down clothing of the whites. Black and white children customarily played together in the dust before the farmhouse door.

These small slave-holding families were by no means wealthy. Men, women, and children, both black and white, worked hard to keep the farm going. They ate simple food: fried pork, corn bread, molasses, vegetables, and fruit only in season. Black children received little or no schooling, but the children of these small slaveholders did not get much more: many whites in the South of the time could not read or write. From the viewpoint of today, it does not appear many whites were materially much better off than blacks.

There was of course one very significant difference: whites were free, blacks were not. Blacks were serving life sentences in open-air prisons that they could not leave without permission, obeying orders from sunup to sundown. They could be—and often were—lashed, sometimes until their backs were masses of raw meat. Not all masters were free with the lash, nor were all cruel to their slaves. But many were. We should not have any illusions of happy-go-lucky blacks devoted to their kindly old "massas," but we should understand that in much of the South blacks and whites were intermingled, and lived lives that were quite similar. Until the beginning of the nineteenth century, blacks and whites worshiped in the same churches, where they listened to the same sermons about hellfire and damnation and sang the same hymns. They developed a lot of the same habits, speech patterns, held many of the same superstitions, believed in the same myths. There were differences, of course: each had rituals that were special to them. But the culture they shared was large.

Inevitably, blacks learned the European music of their masters. On the big plantations sometimes a talented slave or two was trained to play dance music for the slave owners and their guests. Especially in the North, there existed small numbers of free blacks, some of whom became professional musicians. The most famous of these musicians was a man called Frank Johnson, who composed a lot of music, led a very popular concert orchestra, and in 1837 gave a concert in England for Queen Victoria.

Blacks, thus, learned European music. But they had a natural tendency to bring into it some elements drawn from African music. This sort of thing, the melding of elements from different cultures to create something new, is called *syncretism*. A good example of syncretism is the way blacks in America fused the Christian religion of the Europeans with African ways of worship. Blacks prayed to Jesus and the God of the Bible, and sang the familiar Christian hymns. But they also danced and sang in church in a manner similar to the ritual dances of West Africa.

In the same fashion blacks syncretized African and European music. African music, we remember, was built around *polyrhythms*, that is to say, two and frequently more beats going along at once. European music was much less subtle rhythmically but more complex harmonically. Where the essence of African music lay in the rhythms, the essence of European music was in melody and harmony.

Despite their differences, the two types of music had many similarities. For one, the African scale is basically not much different from the familiar European *do-re-mi* scale. On the other side of the coin, there is plenty of rhythm in European music, especially in the stirring music of marches, or the lively music meant for dancing, for of course Europeans, like most peoples everywhere, danced.

So the possibility of combining the two was there, and that is what blacks in America did. Analyzing the way blacks melded African and European music is not easy, but we can see at least three things. One was that blacks sang and played the European hymns and dance tunes with a rhythmic lilt that had not been there before. It was not exactly the polyrhythms of African music; however, blacks seemed to sing some of the notes a little bit ahead of or behind where they would normally fall, so that they caught you by surprise. This gave something of the effect of two different beats going on at once.

Blacks also sang some of the notes of the scale a little flat by European standards. This was particularly true of the third and seventh notes of the *do-re-mi* scale—that is, *mi* and *ti*. This was not a matter of error but simply because that was the way those notes were sung in African music.

Finally, they made a practice of changing the sound of the music at points of heightened intensity. They might introduce what is called *melisma*, that is, a sudden flurry of quick little notes. They might coarsen the tone with a guttural sound. Or they might use falsetto, that is, jump the melody way up to the tops of their voices. Once again, these practices were modifications of devices found in African music. By the early part of the nineteenth century, if not before, blacks in America had created a new kind of music that had never existed before by crushing together African and European forms and devices—a music that was neither European nor African but something of its own. Blacks sang this new type of music at work, in churches in the form of hymns, and to dance to in the evenings by the cabins or around the fires at turpentine camps.

This new music was different, but not so different that whites could not understand it. It was a little strange, a little unusual, but not entirely foreign, and very quickly whites grew interested in it. Frequently they would go out to the cabins to watch the slaves dance, and hear the music. Indeed, it became a custom to take visitors, especially from the North, to visit the slave cabins for the music and dancing. At times they would even join in the dancing. Other whites would go to black churches to enjoy the music there.

This interest in black music became a boom, a fad, after about 1830, with the development of what came to be called the *minstrel show*. These were variety shows put on by white performers with their faces blacked up with burnt cork or greasepaint. Minstrel shows offered songs, dances, and comedy that were purported to have been taken directly from the slave quarters of the plantations. Actually, these so-called plantation melodies were substantially modified versions of true black music. The off-pitch notes were changed to make them fit with the European scale, and the rhythmic lilt was simulated by the use of what musicians call dotted rhythms. (The first four notes of "Turkey in the Straw" are a good example of the basic rhythm used in these plantation melodies.)

The most famous composer of plantation songs was Stephen Foster, whose tunes like "My Old Kentucky Home," and "De Camptown Races," were very popular. Another important composer of these songs was James A. Bland, a black, who wrote "Carry Me Back to Old Virginny," and "Oh, Dem Golden Slippers."

After the Civil War, blacks began to put on minstrel shows of their own, ironically blacking up to stay within the minstrel tradition. From this point forward blacks increasingly moved into the entertainment business, performing as singers, dancers, and comedians in the variety or vaudeville shows that were the main form of popular entertainment

THE CRADLE OF JAZZ

17

The Fisk Jubilee Singers made a number of tours in the United States beginning in the early 1870s. They were very popular and created the vogue for what were called "Negro Spirituals," songs like "Swing Low, Sweet Chariot," which are still sung today. Interest in the spiritual helped to popularize black musical forms, opening the way for jazz.

until about 1920. These black performers brought to their work elements drawn from their own tradition of song, dance, and humor.

Beginning in the 1870s, a group of singers from Fisk University, one of the first black colleges, started to tour America, singing versions of "spirituals" from their own churches. Once again, these songs were modified to make them fit better into the European style. The spirituals quickly became widely popular, to the point where pieces like "Go Down Moses" and "Ezekiel Saw De Wheel" were as well known to whites as they were to blacks.

By the end of the nineteenth century white Americans were very familiar with black music in the modified form of plantation songs, spirituals, and tunes blacks were singing in vaudeville. Thus they were prepared for yet another version of black music when it burst upon the scene in the late 1890s. This was ragtime. Exactly where ragtime came from nobody is sure. It may have been born when blacks attempted to transfer their banjo music to the piano, but this is only a guess. The essential element in ragtime was *syncopation*. The word means to place a note in between the beats. Syncopation has always been quite common in European music—there is plenty of it in the music of Bach, for example. But ragtime carried syncopation to an extreme. The basic scheme was for the right hand to play a lot of fast, highly syncopated figures, while the left hand beat out a steady "oompah" bass. The incessant syncopation gave the music the ragged rhythmic feel that is its primary quality. Ragtime quickly became popular in the United States. It was not only played by pianists, but was arranged for dance bands, and was even played by the big brass bands that were important to popular music of the time.

By far the most famous of the ragtimers was Scott Joplin. The son of a slave, he was born in Texas to parents with a strong interest in music. They were able to arrange for him to have music lessons. He quickly showed great talent in both classical and popular music. While still a teenager, he left home to work as an itinerant musician. He landed in St. Louis in about 1890, where he found the new ragtime music just aborning. Scott Joplin became its master. In 1899 he published a piece called "Maple Leaf Rag," which soon became the most famous of rags. Joplin later wrote an opera and a ballet. Neither were very successful, and it is for his wonderful rags that he is today most remembered.

But ragtime was not jazz. Something more had to be brought to the mix. It is probable that a good many people from various groups contributed to the making of jazz, but it does seem clear that key to the process was a group of people today called Creoles. (The term is somewhat confusing and has had different meanings at various times.) The Creoles were a people of mixed blood who had a unique culture of their own. Many of these "Creoles of color," as they were sometimes

Scott Joplin was one of the first, and certainly the most famous, of the ragtime composers. He considered his music an art form to be taken as seriously as classical music. *Courtesy of the New York Public Library.*

called, were descended from mixed-blood people who fled to Louisiana from Haiti because of internal turmoil there between 1800 and 1810.

The culture of these Creoles of color was significantly different from both the black and white cultures surrounding them. The Creoles spoke French, not English; were Catholics, not Protestants; were not day laborers as most blacks were, but owned small businesses like shops and bakeries, or worked at skilled trades, such as bricklaying and carpentry. They were, furthermore, rather clannish, sticking to themselves rather than mingling with the people around them.

The Creoles clung to certain aspects of the old African culture more than other blacks. For example, although they were basically Catholics and attended the traditional mass, many were also involved with an African-based religion called *Vodoun*, or *Voodoo*.

Creole music came out of the people's French ancestry, and was quite European generally, much more so than the music of the black spiritual and work song. Indeed, many Creole musicians were trained in European classical music, and played in small symphony orchestras. Nonetheless, there was in their folk music a peculiar rhythmic lilt that was somehow different from the rhythmic feel of other types of music around them. It is a good guess that these mixed-blood Creoles, from a culture that as late as 1900 still contained African elements, a lot of them living out in country towns west of New Orleans, played an important role in the creation of jazz.

One of the best of these early Creole jazz musicians was Edward "Kid" Ory. He was born about 1890 in La Place, a country town near Lake Pontchartrain, about thirty miles west of New Orleans. He played several instruments, but his main one was the trombone. He formed his own band when he was in his early teens, using cornet, trombone, violin, string bass, guitar, and drums. The band played a very rough sort of jazz, but was successful, especially playing for dances. Ory had his

THE CRADLE OF JAZZ

21

heart set on moving the group to New Orleans, where there was glamour and money to be made, but his parents insisted that he stay at home until he was twenty-one. On his twenty-first birthday he departed for New Orleans, where he formed his first band. By 1913 the Ory group was considered the best jazz band in New Orleans, which really meant the world. At various times Ory had such important early jazz players as cornetist Joseph "King" Oliver, and clarinetists Lawrence Duhé and Johnny Dodds in his band. In 1918 Oliver was replaced by Louis Armstrong, giving the great jazzman his first important job.

In 1919 Ory migrated to California where a number of New Orleanian musicians were living. The band he formed there became one of the best, and it made the first true jazz records cut by a black group. Ory was one of the best of the early jazz trombonists, and also a composer of excellent jazz tunes of the type then played, like "Ory's Creole Trombone," "Savoy Blues," and "Muskrat Ramble," even today a standard with New Orleans–style bands.

Even more important than Ory was another Creole about his age or perhaps a little older, Ferdinand "Jelly Roll" Morton. Much of the information we have about Morton came from himself and is suspect. It seems clear, however, that his father was F. P. La Menthe, his mother Louise Monette. La Menthe was a builder of some sort, but also a gambler and a good-time sort of person, and he left Louise—or was thrown out by her—when their son was still a boy. She then married a man named Morton, whose name Jelly took. Music was important to Creole families, but they wanted their children to study classical music, not ragtime or the blues. Morton began drumming, using a pair of chair rungs and a tin pan, graduated to the harmonica, then studied the guitar, and finally the piano. He was beginning to develop some skill when, at the age of about fourteen, his mother died. He and his two younger sisters were then brought up by a grandmother.

By this time Jelly Roll was out at night a lot, wandering around the entertainment district of the city. New Orleans was, and is, very much

Basin Street ran along one side of the famous New Orleans entertainment district, Storyville. Contrary to what is widely believed, not much jazz was played in Storyville. However, Tom Anderson's club, at left, used many of the young jazz musicians of the time, among them Louis Armstrong.

a good-time town, always attracting a lot of tourists and people with money to spend. The entertainment district of the city was afloat then with gamblers, entertainers, toughs, and millionaires, mingling indiscriminately in the saloons, cabarets, and dance halls of the area. Everyone was dressed in the most colorful clothes—red-and-white-striped shirts, green derby hats, shoes with lightbulbs in the toes that winked off and on.

Music was everywhere. Even the dingiest, dirtiest saloon had at least a piano player whacking away at ragtime or a blues guitarist singing his lament. Many of the places had full-fledged bands playing the new hot music that was just aborning.

Jelly threw himself into this exciting world. He was careful, however, to keep his grandmother from knowing what he was doing, and explained that he was out late at night because he had a job as a night watchman at a factory. Very quickly he began to get jobs playing for

THE CRADLE OF JAZZ

various establishments in the entertainment district. He was by no means an accomplished player; but at a time when there were no records, no radio, and all music was live, musicians who could play even a little could earn some money.

Jelly knew his limitations, and put himself under the guidance of a pianist named Tony Jackson, an all-around entertainer who could sing, play classical music as well as ragtime and popular tunes, and who also

Jelly Roll Morton's claim that he invented jazz is not true, but he played a considerable role in shaping it. He left New Orleans and by the 1920s was in Chicago, making records and playing in clubs there. Morton was considered the best pianist in jazz at the time. *Courtesy of the New York Public Library.*

wrote such hit songs as "Pretty Baby," which is sometimes still played today. He also listened to a blues pianist well known in the area named Mamie Desdoumes, another Creole. Mamie Desdoumes was missing two fingers on her right hand, and only knew one blues tune, but Jelly would later say, "Mamie first really sold me on the blues."

By his late teens Morton was improving and beginning to make a mark for himself. Then early one morning, as he was coming home from a job in the entertainment district, his grandmother spotted him. He was dressed in his finest clothes, and she knew immediately that he had not been working as a night watchman. She told him right then and there that he could not live in their house anymore, for as an entertainer, he was not fit to associate with his two younger sisters. Jelly was badly hurt, and it was some time before he got over it. But whether he liked it or not, he was now on his own.

He began to travel, first up and down the coast of the Gulf of Mexico to towns like Biloxi, Mississippi, and Mobile, Alabama. Eventually he worked his way out to the West Coast, and finally to Chicago, where he began to make a long series of classic jazz recordings—some piano solos and some with his band the Red Hot Peppers. His compositions for this group are considered among the greatest in the original New Orleans style.

Jelly Roll Morton was the first truly significant jazz pianist, and he influenced many others. He was a master of the blues, but could also play in the complex stride style, a jazz version of ragtime. As in ragtime, stride used the "oompah" bass, in which the pianist struck a note, an octave on the first and third beats of each measure, and a full chord on the alternate beats. This system gave the music a strong, rocking, freight-train propulsion. With his right hand the stride pianist played rapid figures often repeated up and down the keyboard. One of the main creators of stride was a New Jerseyan, James P. Johnson; but Morton was playing the stride style quite early himself. He always said that a pianist ought to imitate a band, and in his work you can hear reflections of trombones in his left hand, clarinets in his right.

Life was difficult for blacks in the early days of jazz, especially for one who was handicapped. One way for a blind person to make a living was through music. Blind Lemon Jefferson began singing on street corners, then went on to record and play in clubs. He is today considered one of the finest of the early "country" blues singers.

Other of these young Creoles in the first generation of jazz musicians were cornetists Freddie Keppard and Buddie Petit; bassist and guitarist Bill Johnson; trombonist Honoré Dutrey; and clarinetists Jimmie Noone and Sidney Bechet.

These Creoles were not alone in inventing jazz. Other blacks were important, too. Cornetist Joe "King" Oliver was one of the first to use the plunger mute, and even used bottles and ashtrays to produce the "wah-wah" effect. Bunk Johnson was considered by some to be as good as any of the cornetists of the earliest times, playing a clean, simple style with a sweet tone. Drummer Baby Dodds and his brother, clarinetist Johnny Dodds would, a few years later, become very influential.

Some New Orleans whites, like trombonist Tom Brown and his brother, bassist Steve, got interested in the new hot music as it popped

A typical early New Orleans jazz band. Instrumentation in these bands did vary, but the instrumentation shown here was very common. Buddie Petit, the cornetist, was the leader of this group. The clarinet player is Edmund Hall, who went on to become one of the best of the Dixieland clarinetists during the 1940s and after. At left, the singer holds a megaphone, which helped to carry his voice in a crowded dance hall at a time when there were no microphones.

its head up in New Orleans and also became influential. We cannot say that Creoles alone invented jazz, but they did play a leading role.

What we can be sure of is that, however they came to it, white teenagers were forming jazz bands from almost the beginning. By the 1910–1915 period there were a number of jazz bands playing around New Orleans, some of them composed of whites, some of them a mix of Creoles and blacks. These young musicians looked for work wherever they could find it. Jelly Roll Morton, as we have seen, was wandering up and down the Gulf coast picking up jobs. In 1907 the Creole bassist and guitar player Bill Johnson went out to the West Coast and formed a band mainly of New Orleanian Creoles that was quite successful working in San Francisco and Los Angeles. In about 1914 he

In the early days many jazz bands played in vaudeville shows as one of many variety acts. The music was often presented for its comical effects. In this picture the band is backing a pair of comics.

brought out from New Orleans Freddie Keppard, then considered the hottest of the New Orleanian cornetists. This band played tours of vaudeville theaters, traveling to Chicago and New York, where it played the fancy Wintergarden Theatre in 1915.

In the same year a group led by trombonist Tom Brown was booked into Lamb's Cafe, a well-known Chicago club. The band was successful there and moved on to New York. Two or three other groups came up from New Orleans to Chicago to fill the gap. Jazz was becoming known around the nation.

Then, in 1917, a group called the Original Dixieland Jazz Band was booked into the prestigious Reisenweber's in New York. New York was the show business capital of America. The band was written up in the newspapers and soon made some records for Victor (now RCA). These records became instant best-sellers. Jazz was on its way.

CHAPTER 3

THE COMING OF THE JAZZ SOLO

When we think about jazz, the picture that comes immediately to mind is of the jazz soloist—somebody like the saxophonist Lester Young standing in front of the Count Basie band playing chorus after chorus of hot music while the band swings behind him. Jazz heroes today are not the composers and arrangers so much as the soloists, like saxophonists Wayne Shorter and Phil Woods. Certainly the most influential players in jazz almost always have been the great soloists—John Coltrane, Miles Davis, Benny Goodman—whom thousands of young aspiring musicians set out to emulate.

It is therefore surprising that at the beginning there were very few solos in the music. It was mostly played *ensemble*, that is to say, with all the instruments playing at once in some organized—or, perhaps in the early rough bands, only semiorganized—fashion.

The reason was this: at that time, one of the most popular kinds of music in the United States was brass band music. Actually, the "brass" bands included clarinets, flutes, drums, and cymbals, as well as brass instruments like cornets, trombones, tubas, and various other horns. These bands were very similar to the modern bands we see at football games and in parades today—indeed, such bands of our times are descended directly from the brass band, such as the one led by John Philip Sousa, which might have had as many as fifty musicians, although that was unusual. Most ordinary brass bands consisted of ten to fifteen instruments. A typical band would have two or three cornets, two or three clarinets and fifes, one or two trombones, two alto or tenor horns, a tuba, one or two snare drums, and a bass drum with a cymbal mounted on the drum.

There were thousands of such bands in the United States. They were found everywhere. Many of them were organized by the members of clubs, unions, people working in factories, groups like the Boy

The Reliance Brass Band was typical of the small bands that evolved into jazz groups. This group was not a true jazz band but played for shows and parades. Note how young the musicians are, many of them still teenagers.

Scouts and the Elks Club. Units of the army, navy, and marine corps often had their own bands—during the Civil War each side had hundreds of bands whose members had to put down their instruments and fight from time to time. And of course there were bands that were organized solely because the members wanted a chance to play.

These brass bands played for all sorts of occasions. Since you could not get music by pressing a button or flicking a switch, people would whistle or sing as they worked. They would gather around the upright piano or pump organ in the evening and harmonize old favorites. And of course they would put together little bands for dances or just for fun. Today, because we have so much professional music available to us, we don't make very much of it ourselves. In those days singing came naturally to almost everybody simply because they had sung from childhood. Most ordinary people knew harmony parts to dozens of songs, and many could easily work out the harmonies to ones they did not know. Making music was something that Americans did without thinking much about it, as we today take it for granted that we can play sports.

Brass bands were much in demand. Many of the villages and towns in which the majority of Americans of the time lived had little wooden bandstands in the center of town, where the local brass band would give Sunday concerts in good weather. Such bands played in parades on the Fourth of July, Memorial Day, and other national holidays. But they also played hymns at funerals, popular songs and rags at dances, and even excerpts from symphonies and operas at concerts.

These bands did not improvise. They played from written music, and there was a huge music publishing industry to supply scores and arrangements of any kind of music for any combination of instruments. Some of this music, like that played by the famous Sousa band, was very difficult, and needed virtuosi to play it, like the famous trombonist Arthur Pryor. Other pieces were meant for beginners, and were simple.

Brass bands did at times allow one or two of their best musicians to step forward and play solo. Showy cornet solos of perhaps a well-known operatic aria were especially popular, and the virtuoso soloist was expected to embellish his solo with all sorts of fancy "turns" he invented or learned from books of embellishments. But for the most part brass bands played ensemble as they do in parades today.

The first jazz bands were offshoots of the brass bands. As was true elsewhere in the United States, New Orleans, and the country towns around that city, had scores of brass bands. Indeed, in New Orleans they were everywhere. The New Orleans guitarist Danny Barker described it this way:

> One of my pleasantest memories as a kid growing up in New Orleans was how a bunch of us kids, playing, would suddenly hear sounds. It was like a phenomenon, like the Aurora Borealis—maybe. The sound of men playing would be so clear, but we wouldn't be sure where it was coming from. So we'd start trotting, start running—"It's this way! It's that way!" And sometimes, after running for awhile, you'd find you'd be nowhere near that music. But that music could come on you any time like that. The city was full of the sounds of music (Nat Shapiro and Nat Hentoff, *Hear Me Talkin' to Ya* [New York: Dover Publications, 1955], 3).

When Kid Ory or King Oliver were organizing their first bands, they based them on the brass bands. Actually, these first little jazz groups were not entirely in the tradition of the brass band, for they also drew on another very popular type of musical group, the string band. A string band might consist of three to seven guitars, banjos, string basses, and violins. The early jazz bands sometimes used a guitar, a bass, or a violin—or perhaps all three, as Kid Ory's first band did.

But the brass band was the basis of the first jazz bands, and as we have seen, brass band music was largely ensemble, with solos few and far between. And that is why jazz at first was not a soloist's music.

The music played by those kids in that sunlit barn—or the Ory group, for that matter—generally followed the pattern of brass band

String bands were very popular in the United States during the time when jazz was growing up. They were often used in restaurants to provide soft music for dining but might appear anywhere, as at this sporting event. In the early days many jazz bands included violins as well as guitars, banjos, and string basses.

music. The cornet played the melody, or the "lead," the drums, bass, and guitar beat out the rhythm, and the trombone, clarinet, and other horns played supporting parts—at times they might harmonize the melody or they might play little rhythmic figures; frequently they would play countermelodies. The trombonist especially would fit figures in between the phrases of the main melody to tie them together, sometimes slurring from note to note.

Surprisingly, the music of these first young jazz musicians was not really improvised. Today we see improvisation as the heart and soul of jazz, and we find it hard to imagine jazz that was not made up spontaneously on the spot. But these musicians were coming out of the brass band tradition. Their aim was for each member of the band to work out a part for himself that fit, and then to play it more or less the same each time. Of course there was variation. Nobody was required to play the notes exactly the same every time; you could make changes here and there if you felt like it. Furthermore, that indefinable lilt, that swing, that was so critical to jazz, depended on notes being a little out of joint with the beat, a little ahead of or behind where they would be found traditionally. This rhythmic lilt had to be felt at the moment. But basically this early jazz was planned, not improvised.

How, then, did jazz get turned on its head, to make the solo, rather than the ensemble, the central point? Because recordings from this era are so spotty, it is difficult to be sure who began emphasizing solo

The saxophone ultimately came to be seen as the jazz instrument par excellence, and many of the great jazz soloists have been saxophonists. But the instrument was late in coming to jazz and was not established until the late 1920s. Before that it had been seen as a novelty instrument, frequently used in vaudeville. This vaudeville group from about 1910 shows a whole family of saxophones.

playing, but the evidence points to Sidney Bechet, another Creole from the New Orleans French Quarter. Bechet was, quite simply, a prodigy. His older brother, Leonard, played clarinet. According to Sidney's own story, he began sneaking Leonard's instrument out of the bureau drawer where he kept it and learned how to play. When he was only seven or eight years old, it happened that some older musicians, not much more than teenagers themselves, came over to the Bechet house to jam. Leonard was not there, so Sidney slipped out the clarinet and began to play along with the others in another room. The older musicians were astonished to hear this fine clarinet playing coming through the air, and were even more astonished to discover that the player was Leonard's kid brother, Sidney.

Thereafter some of these musicians began using Sidney on their regular jobs. By the time he was a teenager he was a legend among the jazz musicians of the city, and in 1919, when he was just out of his teens, he was hired by the noted black bandleader Will Marion Cook to make a tour of England with his Southern Syncopated Orchestra. This was not a jazz band but a concert group. However, Bechet was featured with a solo in the blues, which impressed everybody who heard it. When he returned to New York he quickly made a name for himself as the shining star of the new music—among musicians, at least, if not with the general public. Soon he started to record with a black bandleader and record producer named Clarence Williams under various names, including the Clarence Williams Blue Five, and the Red Onion Jazz Babies. Two of these sides, "Kansas City Man" and "Wildcat Blues," in particular excited a lot of young jazz musicians taken with the fervor of Bechet's playing.

Sometime around 1920 Bechet discovered the soprano saxophone, which had a larger sound. Gradually it became his primary instrument, although he continued to play the clarinet through most of his life.

Sidney Bechet was, even more than most jazz musicians, a man who marched to his own drummer—a fractious individual who went his own way, getting into a good many arguments in the process. He was com-

JAZZ: AN AMERICAN SAGA

Sidney Bechet with his mighty soprano saxophone in the 1940s. He was by this time rising in popularity in America but would soon move to France, where he became even more popular, having a street named for him after his death. *Courtesy of William P. Gottlieb.*

petitive, not by nature somebody who fit comfortably into a cooperative ensemble. He always wanted to be the dominant player. Thus, while he was theoretically playing a part in the standard New Orleans ensemble, he was often so far out front as to make it seem that he was soloing.

His style of playing also made it appear that he was improvising, but it is difficult to know how much of his music was planned and how much was improvised. It was probably a good deal of both. However, there can be no doubt about the quality of his playing. He was a very inventive, hot, driving player with a large, dominating sound, especially on soprano saxophone. He impressed everyone who heard him at this time. Duke Ellington once called him the "greatest of all originators."

Because Bechet was so much of a wanderer, spending a good deal of the 1920s in Europe, he did not record nearly as much as he might have had he stayed in New York, where the recording industry was based. Nonetheless, records like "Wildcat Blues" and others he made at this time were influential. Bechet may not have invented the improvised jazz solo, but he was probably the first to show what could be done with it.

Another musician who was key in turning jazz from an ensemble to a soloist's music was Louis Armstrong, one of the most celebrated musicians in jazz. During his lifetime he was the subject of thousands of newspaper and magazine stories, appeared in over fifty movies, was one of the first blacks in America to have his own radio show, and, by the later stages of his career, had become an international show business star.

Unfortunately, a great deal of what has been written about Armstrong is myth, as is frequently the case with great heroes. We can be sure, however, that he was raised in great deprivation. He was born, probably, in 1901. His father abandoned the family before he was born, although Louis later lived with him for a brief period as a teenager. His mother loved him, but she often wandered away for days at a time, leaving young Louis to care for his baby sister. They were incredibly poor: Armstrong went barefoot winter and summer, owned most of the time a single pair of pants and a couple of shirts, and sometimes scrambled through garbage cans looking for supper.

Finally, when he was perhaps thirteen, he was put in a home for children from troubled families, known as the Jones Home. Here he joined the band. His natural genius for music came out, and he soon became the cornet star of the group. When he left the Jones Home he

Louis Armstrong in the brass band of the Colored Waif's Home, always known as the Jones Home after the man who organized it. Most of the boys in a band of this kind could not read music and had to pick up their parts by ear. Armstrong got his first training in this band. *Courtesy of the Institute of Jazz Studies, Rutgers University.*

started playing around New Orleans, using borrowed horns because he could not afford to buy a cornet of his own. He played in rough clubs and dance halls in the tough neighborhood he lived in, learning the blues and simple popular tunes. He attached himself to King Oliver, then one of the best-known cornetists in New Orleans. When Oliver moved north to Chicago, Louis replaced him in Kid Ory's band. His reputation rose every year, and in 1922 Oliver brought him up to Chicago to join his well-known Creole Jazz Band.

There was not much soloing in the Creole Jazz Band, but the few solos Armstrong takes, especially one on "Froggie Moore," a Jelly Roll Morton tune, show that he was already playing with a kind of swing

A very rare picture of Louis Armstrong with his mother and his sister, Beatrice. By the time of this picture, Armstrong was beginning to make money as a musician and could afford good clothes, which he had never had as a child.

that none of the other members of the band—and few musicians in jazz—had acquired. Indeed, only Sidney Bechet and Jelly Roll Morton could play with this loose, springy swing.

Armstrong left Oliver in 1924 to spend a year with a band in New York, where he dazzled musicians there with his great powers of invention, his swing, and his astonishing technique. He returned to Chicago in 1925 and began to cut a series of records under his own name, generally lumped together as the Hot Five series. At first these recordings were in the New Orleans style, with a lot of ensemble and limited soloing. But as time went on it became clear to the record company that Armstrong was the selling point. Increasingly these records became features for him, with the other players receding further and further into the background.

Armstrong also began singing on these Hot Five records. His voice was rough, but his innate musicality attracted listeners. He sang more and more, until he was singing on nearly all of his numbers.

But to jazz people it was his trumpet playing that counted. (He switched from cornet to trumpet during the Hot Five.) He had it all— a great imagination that allowed him again and again to produce startling new phrases; a golden, warm, rich tone; speed; a crisp attack; majestic high notes; and above all, that indefinable thing that captures the listener's heart. And unlike many players who have only one story to tell, Louis Armstrong exhibited in his playing great emotional variety, ranging from the wistful "Savoy Blues," to the romping "Hotter Than That," the melancholy, "Tight Like This," and the tragic "West End Blues."

This latter piece is one of the great masterpieces in jazz. It begins with a brilliantly conceived introduction leading into a touching melody. The last chorus is again a solo for Armstrong. He opens it with a note held for almost four measures, which suddenly breaks off into complex, dashing figures and then into a quiet, slow, heartrending close. With records like "West End Blues," Armstrong showed that a jazz solo could be truly fine music. Young jazz musicians of the time were telling themselves, if it feels like this to hear such music, what must it feel like to make it? From this time on, learning how to play solos, not how to manage the ensemble, was the aim of most young, aspiring jazz musicians.

There was more to the switch from the ensemble to the solo style than simply the examples of Sidney Bechet and Louis Armstrong. It is one thing for musicians to work out a new way of playing; it is another to find an audience for it. If American jazz fans had preferred the old New Orleans ensemble to the new solo style, the music would have remained as it had been for a generation. But Americans were ready for the jazz solo. Why?

The answer has to do with sweeping changes in how people in the United States—and in Europe, too—were beginning to think, feel,

The famous King Oliver's Creole Jazz Band. Jazz was frequently presented as comedy, with the players taking foolish positions with their instruments, which they did not, of course, do when they were playing at a dance. Armstrong is out front with a slide cornet. He really played a regular cornet, seen on the floor in front of him.

and act. In the nineteenth century the United States had been dominated by an ethical system that came to be called "Victorianism," after
Queen Victoria, who ruled England for much of the century. People
were not supposed to drink much, and many did not drink at all. Sex
was never mentioned. Even dancing was frowned on by many people.
Duty, responsibility, and sacrificing for others were the key rules.
Everything in life was affected. For example, females of all ages could
not sprawl back in a chair, gesticulate, sit with their legs crossed. They
had to sit upright, with their arms kept close to their bodies. Males
were allowed a little more leeway but not much more. People's dress
was very conservative, with women wearing skirts that came down to
their ankles, men wearing suits with vests and neckties not only at
their offices but often at baseball games and on picnics. Of course, not
everybody could live up to this social code, but many did and most
people tried.

All of this may sound very disagreeable, but there was a very good
side to Victorianism, too. It emphasized kindness, consideration for
others, putting your family and your community ahead of your own
needs. In many ways the Victorians created a better world than the
one we have today. There was far less crime, far less drug abuse, far
fewer disrupted families. The problem was that the Victorians took the
cry for order and decorum too far. It was a hard code to live up to, and
many people felt repressed under it.

By 1900 or so a lot of people, especially young people, were growing very restless under the Victorian hand. And by 1910 to 1915 some
of them were in open revolt. A new idea was spreading, at first among
intellectuals, writers, and artists, and then out to the populace in general. This was the theory that people ought to be free to express themselves. They ought to be spontaneous, emotional, outgoing, saying
what they felt like saying, doing what their feelings told them to do.

This was all to the good, but once again people took it too far.
What began as a call for more freedom and expressiveness turned into
pure selfishness, the "me-first" ethic, which said that you could do

By the 1950s Armstrong had become the most famous jazz musician in the world, traveling around the globe with his band. Many jazz fans were disappointed that he concentrated on his singing and seemed to have little new to say on his trumpet, but millions of pop music fans were entranced by his winning personality and rough vocal style.

whatever you wanted, regardless of how it might hurt your family, friends, and community.

But that did not happen immediately. This new anti-Victorian spirit of freedom and expressiveness was only beginning to spread through American society in the years when jazz was becoming popular. Not surprisingly, young people imbued with the new idea of freedom and expressiveness were attracted to jazz. It seemed to spring spontaneously from the heart, to be the open expression of feeling, and thus fit exactly with the new attitude sweeping America. It is also not surprising that those opposed to the new way of thinking also opposed jazz—it seemed to them to represent disorder and frenzy rather than Victorian ideals of duty and social responsibility.

But the Victorians were in retreat. By the time Louis Armstrong's Hot Five recordings were coming out in the late 1920s, the new spirit had taken over. An age of *individualism*, in which the needs of each person were seen as more important than the needs of the community, had arrived. And what fit better with individualism than the jazz soloist standing up in front of his band and improvising spontaneously from his feelings?

It was not that the new solo style was necessarily better than the old New Orleans ensemble. Indeed, many jazz fans and musicians preferred the old style, and some, like Jelly Roll Morton and King Oliver, tried to stick to it even when it went out of fashion. New Orleans jazz—or "Dixieland" jazz, as it is called today—is still a very good form of music. But the solo style fit the new spirit of the times better. It came to stay; and the age it was born in, the 1920s, came to be known as the Jazz Age.

One instrument that benefited a great deal from the new interest in the jazz solo was the piano. Most soloists needed some sort of accompaniment, but the pianist could stand all by himself. Some of the first jazz piano solos were recorded by Jelly Roll Morton in 1923, in his

James P. Johnson is often called the "Father of Stride" piano. Others helped in the development of the style, but Johnson was its first great master.

style that combined stride and the blues. Earl "Fatha" Hines made an important set of piano solos for the little-known QRS label in 1928. But the jazz piano really came into its own during the swing era. Among those who did a great deal to popularize the piano was Thomas "Fats" Waller. He had studied with the stride pioneer, James P. Johnson, and had quickly mastered the style. In addition to his brilliant piano playing, Waller was also a fine singer and popular entertainer with a happy-go-lucky manner. Through the 1930s and into the 1940s he made hundreds of recordings—some of them solos, some with his own small group—most of them featuring his singing and playing.

Even more influential than Waller was Teddy Wilson, who began playing in the manner of Earl Hines. He soon developed a more spare and delicate style, which nonetheless swung very hard. Wilson came to prominence with the Benny Goodman trios and quartets, which were extremely popular during the swing era. Soon young pianists all over the United States were trying to play like Teddy Wilson.

Another pianist who has always astonished musicians was Art Tatum. He went blind as a small boy, took up the piano, and by the time he was a teenager had developed a technique that astounded even masterful classical pianists. Tatum's style was busy and rich, full of complex runs that most other pianists could not get through. He did not have as many followers as Wilson had because few pianists could

Johnson taught Thomas "Fats" Waller the stride style. Waller went on to become widely popular in the United States for his comic singing and patter. Jazz has always had one foot in show business; Waller was able to demonstrate that you could play good jazz and still entertain large audiences.

play many of his figures at the speed he liked, but he is still considered one of the giants of jazz.

Hines, Waller, Tatum, and Wilson developed the jazz piano style, and even after modern jazz came along, younger pianists like Bud Powell played in a similar way, although with modern harmonies. Then, in the 1950s and '60s, Bill Evans, first as a member of Miles

Bud Powell helped to create the bop piano style, building on the work of Teddy Wilson. He could play with the lightning speed bop often required. He used a minimum of chording in the left hand to stay out of the way of the complex harmonies used by bop soloists.

Davis's group, and then with his own trio, produced a different manner. His style was less obviously rhythmic, more subtle and introspective, with much attention paid to sound quality. The Evans style influenced later important pianists like Herbie Hancock and Chick Corea, although they have also forged paths of their own.

Not surprisingly, the rise of interest in solos brought forward the idea of the jazz singer. The earliest jazz recordings, like those of the Original Dixieland Jazz Band, contain no vocals at all. Nor are there any vocals on the famous King Oliver Creole Jazz Band sides.

However, in 1920 a singer called Mamie Smith had a sudden hit with a tune called "Crazy Blues." There had been some popular interest in the blues earlier—W. C. Handy's famous "Memphis Blues" had been published in 1912, before jazz was widely known. With the success of "Crazy Blues," the country was struck by a fad for the blues. Record companies went racing around looking for blues singers to sign up, some of them authentic, many of them not.

Undoubtedly the greatest of these early blues singers was Bessie Smith (no relation to Mamie). She was a big, rough woman with a big, rough voice and an ability to twist the slightly off-pitch blue notes in a way to wring listeners' hearts. We can hear her do this in her classic "St. Louis Blues," accompanied by Louis Armstrong, when she sings "Feelin' *tomorrow*, like I *feel* today." It is as if the weight of the world were on her back.

During the 1920s Bessie Smith earned a great deal of money. When the Great Depression came in 1930 she fell on hard times, as did millions of Americans. By 1937, when the swing bands were catching on and jazz was on the rise again, she tried a comeback. She was touring the South when she was killed in an automobile accident.

Another great jazz singer who lived a tragic life was Billie Holiday. Born exceedingly poor in Baltimore, she was disowned by her father, Clarence Holiday, a guitar player who worked for a time with the pianist and big band leader Fletcher Henderson. Billie moved to New York as a teenager and started out singing in Harlem nightclubs for

Bessie Smith is considered by most jazz critics to be the greatest of all blues singers. She was toughened by her harsh childhood and remained a strong personality throughout her life. Her power comes through clearly in her singing.

nickels and dimes customers threw to her. She was discovered in one of these clubs by a rich jazz fan named John Hammond, who was trying to do what he could for jazz musicians he thought ought to be better known. Hammond arranged for her to make a series of records under the leadership of pianist Teddy Wilson. He also brought in to accompany her many of the leading jazz musicians of the day. These recordings, made from the mid-1930s into the 1940s, are among the most admired records in jazz.

Most of the songs Holiday sang were ordinary popular tunes, but she occasionally sang the blues. Perhaps her best-known blues number is "Fine and Mellow," about a woman pining for her faithless man, which has a haunting quality.

But Billie was able to transform even the sometimes trite popular songs she sang. She took great liberties with the melodies of such

Billie Holiday in the recording studio in the 1950s with two of the finest soloists of the swing era, trumpeter Buck Clayton and alto saxophonist Johnny Hodges. Although Billie looks healthy in this picture, by this time she was beginning to lose her skills through abuse of alcohol and drugs. Nonetheless, she is still considered to be one of the finest jazz singers ever. *Courtesy of CBS.*

songs, often simplifying them considerably, as in "Them There Eyes," where she sings the opening phrase on one note instead of the original four notes written. She was particularly known for her way of phrasing away from the beat, skittering over it as if it did not exist. Even as fine a musician as Teddy Wilson said, "When I play with Billie I have to *count*," in order to keep track of where she was in the song. Sadly, Holiday became addicted to alcohol and drugs, had many unhappy love affairs, and died too young.

Vocals have continued to play a role in jazz, although there is frequently some question as to whether this or that vocalist is truly a jazz singer or a pop singer with jazz inflections. Certainly Louis Armstrong was a pure jazz singer, one of the finest. The very popular "crooner" Bing Crosby could sing excellent jazz when he chose to. Other well-known vocalists who sang jazz were the late Sarah Vaughan and Ella Fitzgerald, and presently Betty Carter and the duo of Roy Kral and Jackie Cain. A great many names could be added to this list.

CHAPTER 4

ALL THOSE
DIFFERENT STYLES

One of the great truths about jazz is that its best practitioners have immediately identifiable ways of playing. Fans, critics, other musicians have no trouble telling, from just a few notes, that a particular solo is by Lester Young or Jack Teagarden or Art Tatum or Roy Eldridge. They recognize the musicians from their approach to harmony, the way they shape their phrases, and from certain figures they employ again and again. Even beginning listeners should very quickly learn to tell the difference between the playing of, for example, Lester Young and Coleman Hawkins, two of the most influential tenor saxophonists in jazz. Young used a light, somewhat dry and airy sound; Hawkins, a rich and at times guttural one; Young stuck to the simplest harmonies; Hawkins liked to use more complicated ones; he divided beats in a very uneven fashion for an emphatic *doodah, doodah* feel; Young divided beats more evenly. Each of these players had his own distinctive style of playing.

That word, *style,* is a very important one to jazz people. As we have seen, *individualism* is very important in jazz. Jazz people will often say,

One of the most individual stylists in jazz was Lester Young, known as "Prez," short for the nickname, "president" of the saxophone, given to him by Billie Holiday. Many other saxophonists tried to imitate Prez, a whole school of them, in fact. But discerning listeners can always tell the real thing. *Courtesy of CBS.*

"So and so has a lot of technique, a pretty sound, but he doesn't have a voice of his own." Most young players begin by imitating an admired idol; but in order to become important musicians they have to develop an individual style of their own that is immediately recognizable.

Style, then, means a great deal to jazz people, and it is therefore not surprising that over the history of the music, a great many verbal wars have been fought over competing styles of jazz. These wars can become quite ferocious, with the defenders of one style attacking loyalists of another quite viciously in print, refusing to speak to each other, and even, on occasion, getting into fistfights over stylistic battles.

These strong loyalties to one style of jazz or another are salutary in some ways, for they call up in jazz fans passion and devotion to their beloved music. Nonetheless, the whole thing is sometimes carried too far, for frequently loyalists become so opposed to competing styles that they cannot see the beauties in them. Not surprisingly, just as we will probably stay loyal to a particular baseball or football team we began to follow when we were young, so, too, do most jazz fans tend to favor throughout their lives the style of jazz they were attracted to when they were first learning about the music.

But really, there is much to be gained from spreading our likes out more broadly. Most of us, for example, prefer certain kinds of books—mysteries, romances, historical fiction, or whatever; but few of us refuse to read anything else. Unfortunately, that is what jazz fans do all too often. Anyone truly interested in jazz, then, ought to know something about the various styles of jazz that have developed over the course of its history.

We have already had a look at the first jazz style—the music that grew up in New Orleans at the very beginning. This music is today most often called Dixieland. It is also sometimes called "New Orleans

An early recording session with Bix Beiderbecke (cornet, standing) at the famous Gennett Studios, where a host of Chicago musicians recorded in the 1920s. The trombone player is Tommy Dorsey, who would become one of the most celebrated bandleaders of the big band era. This was an acoustical recording. There were no microphones; sound entered the horn in the center of the picture, which then carried it to a needle cutting the wax master.

jazz," and, especially in England and other countries, "traditional," or "trad," jazz. (However, the term "traditional jazz" is today sometimes used indiscriminately to lump together a number of earlier jazz styles and can be confusing.) This original jazz, Dixieland, was a contrapuntal music with two or three melody lines running along together with few solos, and it was played with a two-beat rhythmic feel. As played today there are generally more solos, although ensemble playing predominates, and often a four-beat swing rhythm.

Dixieland reached its peak, so far as recordings go, in the mid-1920s with pieces in the Louis Armstrong Hot Five series like "Muskrat Ramble" and "Cornet Chop Suey"; Jelly Roll Morton's Red Hot Peppers' recordings, like "The Chant" and "Sidewalk Blues"; Bix Beiderbecke pieces like "Royal Garden Blues" and "Jazz Me Blues"; and Red Nichols and his Five Pennies' cuts like "Stampede" and "Hurricane."

But change was coming. As has been so often the case in jazz, the influence of a single powerful figure can create shifts in fashion. In this instance the key figure was not a jazz musician, but a trained classical violinist named Paul Whiteman.

The story goes like this. Back in the early days of jazz, dance music was usually provided by small, unsung little groups that frequently consisted of a violin or a cornet supported by a small rhythm section of some combination of drums, piano, and banjo. Indeed, a dance "band" often consisted only of piano and drums. These groups played each song as written two or three times and then went on to the next tune. There were, of course, a few larger and more polished dance groups in operation, but these were mainly put together from time to time for balls at the homes of the wealthy. Most people danced to small, rough groups.

There was obviously room for improvement, and around 1915, out in San Francisco, a young musician named Ferde Grofé saw the possibilities. Grofé, like Whiteman, was a trained classical musician who frequently worked in symphony orchestras. He also tried to make money on the side by playing for dances. It occurred to him that, with his classical training, he could spruce up dance music if he worked out arrangements of tunes, supplying harmonies and countermelodies for three or four instruments. He teamed up with Art Hickman, who was leading a small dance band at the famous Rose Room of the St. Francis Hotel in San Francisco. Very quickly the Hickman orchestra became the rage on the West Coast. The band's Columbia recordings were very successful, and it appeared that Art Hickman was headed for fame. But he was not ambitious, and it was Paul Whiteman who capitalized on the success of the new type of dance orchestra.

Paul Whiteman had a flair for publicity. He hired Grofé to play piano and write arrangements, and he employed musicians who could read Grofé's arrangements quickly. His first recordings for the Victor record label were quite popular, and by the mid-1920s the Whiteman band was as celebrated as the Beatles were to be in their time.

Whiteman adopted the title of "King of Jazz." However, he was by no means a jazz musician, nor was his orchestra truly a jazz band. Nonetheless, it played with a jazz bounce, and contained some very fine jazz soloists, including for a period the great Bix Beiderbecke.

With the success of the Whiteman orchestra, it became clear that the American dancing public preferred the big orchestra, playing from arrangements, to the old Dixieland band with its contrapuntal style. Other bandleaders were swept along: King Oliver added saxophones in 1926, Red Nichols's "Five" Pennies grew to ten, Louis Armstrong began using arrangements for his Hot Five.

One of the most important bandleaders of the period was not originally a jazz musician at all. Fletcher Henderson grew up studying classical music. By 1921 he was in New York working as the musical director for Black Swan, the first black-owned record company. In 1924 he had a chance to take a band into a Broadway nightclub. Henderson quickly teamed up with Don Redman, a conservatory-trained musician, who began writing complex orchestral arrangements in the manner made popular by Grofé when he was with Whiteman. Although neither Redman nor Henderson was a first-class jazz impro-

The 78 rpm records of the early days were ten inches in diameter, made of breakable material, and only played for about three minutes. Records were often issued on several labels under different orchestra names. The Imperial recording of "I'll See You in My Dreams" was made by the Fletcher Henderson Orchestra.

viser, they had some excellent soloists in the band, including saxophonist Coleman Hawkins and trombonist Charlie Green. However, Henderson realized that the public was demanding a hot edge to its dance music, and in 1924, when he started a long engagement at the famous Roseland Ballroom, he brought in Louis Armstrong as a jazz specialist. Armstrong was at this time rapidly maturing into the brilliant improviser he would become, and his solos with Henderson inspired musicians around New York to emulate him. The Henderson band quickly became perhaps the hottest dance band of the moment.

At virtually the same time, a group called the Washingtonians, which had been playing polite cocktail music at a well-known Harlem club, was brought into another Broadway club. The members of the group recognized that they needed to heat up their music for the Broadway crowd and they hired trumpeter Bubber Miley, a follower of King Oliver, and, for a brief period, Sidney Bechet. Miley and Bechet set the example in jazz for the other players in the group. Soon the band's pianist, Duke Ellington, emerged as leader. In 1927 the band got a job at the well-known Cotton Club. The group had to be

At first dance bands were quite small, sometimes consisting of a piano, drums, and a melody instrument like a violin or trumpet. This band, with Duke Ellington at the piano, was fairly large for the time, and consisted of trumpet, trombone, saxophone, piano, and banjo. The group was called the Washingtonians and worked a club on Broadway in New York called the Hollywood Inn.

enlarged for this job and needed a lot of new arrangements, which Ellington set about creating. His brilliance as an arranger and composer shone through, and soon the Duke Ellington Orchestra was one of the best-known jazz bands in America.

One more leader to put together an important band of the period was Jean Goldkette, who had been born in France. Goldkette was originally interested in organizing dance bands on the Whiteman model, but when he saw the demand for jazz, he heated up his group with strong arrangements by Bill Challis and hired top-quality soloists like Bix Beiderbecke, clarinetist Jimmy Dorsey, and guitarist Eddie Lang.

By the late 1920s there existed all over America this new type of jazz band, usually consisting of three trumpets, two trombones, three saxophones, and a rhythm section, although personnel frequently varied. These bands played carefully crafted and well-rehearsed arrangements, interspersed with many jazz solos. Even the arranged passages were written and played with a swing, after the fashion of a jazz solo. Of course these were dance bands, and they had to play a lot of sweet, slow tunes for dancing, even waltzes. But it was the hot pieces that attracted attention. Along the way they created many immortal jazz masterpieces, like Ellington's "Black and Tan Fantasy," "The Mooche," and "Ring Dem Bells"; Henderson's "Sugarfoot Stomp" and "Just Blues"; Goldkette's "Clementine"; the Casa Loma Orchestra's "San Sue Strut"; McKinney's Cotton Pickers' "Zonky"; and hundreds more.

Then, in 1930, America was hit by the greatest financial depression in its history. The record industry collapsed, dance halls and nightclubs snapped shut, and it seemed almost as if jazz were dead, a relic of the good times of the Roaring Twenties. It was not quite dead, however: the Ellington Orchestra, in particular, continued to thrive as its leader produced a steady stream of masterpieces featuring some of

Dance arrangements were built around the interplay of sections of instruments. This is Duke Ellington's famous trombone section of "Tricky Sam" Nanton, Juan Tizol, and Lawrence Brown.

Even when the big bands dominated popular music in America, there was still a taste for small band jazz. Bandlead-ers like Duke Ellington sometimes pulled small groups out of their big bands to play specialty numbers once or twice a night.

the finest soloists in jazz like trumpeter Cootie Williams and alto sax-ophonist Johnny Hodges. But most bands broke up, and musicians found it hard to get work.

Then, in 1934, a clarinetist named Benny Goodman, much admired by musicians for his fine technique and passionate improvis-ing but unknown to the public, decided to start a hot dance band. He was facing serious odds: times were still bad, a quarter of the American population was out of work, and the rest had few pennies to spare for amusement. The record companies wanted only the romantic music they felt Americans preferred during hard times.

But Goodman gathered a group of young musicians who wanted to play hot music and were willing to take a chance. Jobs were hard to get, but in 1935 the band managed to tour across the country. The tour was not a total failure but in many places audiences wanted only sweet music, as the record companies suspected. Goodman thought of giving up the band. Then, that fall the band ended the tour at the Palomar Ballroom in Los Angeles. Goodman was prepared to play out the date and disband. However, on opening night, when the musicians turned up at the ballroom, they found a line of people waiting to get in that ran around the block. They could not believe what they were seeing, and Goodman called for the sweet tunes that audiences seemed to want. The young dancers gave them a lukewarm reception. Suddenly Goodman said to the band, "If we're finished, we might as well go out playing what we want." He called for some of the hot tunes in the band's book, like "Bugle Call Rag" and "King Porter Stomp." The ballroom came alive, the crowd roared. These were the numbers they had been waiting for and before the evening was over the band was a success. Apparently during the time the band had been crossing the country, its records had reached the West Coast and were being played by some disc jockeys. Unbeknownst to Goodman, his band already had a following there.

The huge success of the Goodman band encouraged other bandleaders to jump in, first by twos and threes, then by dozens, and finally by scores. By the end of the 1930s there were hundreds of these "swing" bands playing in America. Among the most famous were the bands of Goodman, Glenn Miller, Jimmy and Tommy Dorsey, Count Basie, Charlie Barnet, Woody Herman, Jimmie Lunceford, and Artie Shaw, and of course the older groups, like Ellington and Casa Loma. Big band swing of the 1930s and the 1940s was not all jazz in the purest sense. These groups had to play a lot of sweet numbers for dancing, usually the popular tunes of the time. But they played a lot of hot numbers in the old formula of hard-swinging arranged passages mixed with hot solos. Among the classics of the style were the Goodman pieces already mentioned, Barnet's "Cherokee," Herman's "Four Brothers," Basie's "Jumping at the Woodside," Lunceford's "White Heat," Tommy Dorsey's "Marie," and many Ellington pieces, such as "Take the A Train" and "Things Ain't What They Used to Be."

The swing-band era collapsed in a rush right after World War II. Many factors were responsible but a change in American taste was probably key. At the moment, Americans had suffered through a terrible depression and an even more terrible war, and they had had enough excitement for a while. They turned to romantic singers of light songs, like Frank Sinatra and Perry Como. A few of the big bands struggled on for a while: Stan Kenton and Woody Herman had considerable success playing a more modern version of swing, and both the Ellington and Basie bands went on for decades until their leaders' deaths. But jazz itself was turning in other directions.

Once again the lead was taken by charismatic figures who have gone on to be regarded with awe by many jazz fans. The first of these was John "Dizzy" Gillespie. Gillespie was a smart, hardworking, very determined young musician. He was, nonetheless, cocky and rebellious, and frequently got himself on the wrong side of the leaders he worked for. He was the sort of musician who liked to go his own way, and when he was still quite young and unknown he was experimenting with harmonies and chords that were novel for jazz. As early as 1939, when swing was at the height of fashion, he began introducing these strange new chords into his solos to the point where one of his bandleaders started calling it "Chinese music."

At the same time, out in Kansas City, an even younger musician was also looking for new ways of playing jazz. Charlie Parker was not merely rebellious but was in many ways perverse, seemingly bound to get himself in trouble with people, which he frequently did. Like Gillespie, he was determined to make a name for himself in jazz. He dropped out of school and struggled with the alto saxophone, at first without much success. But in time, with the help of some older players, he began to master the instrument, and then leaped ahead of the musicians around him into new ways of playing. He was just about twenty when he landed in New York. By this time Gillespie had gathered around him a small coterie of followers to whom he was teaching his new ideas. Some of these people chanced upon Parker, who had

One of the most famous of all jazz bands was the first important bop group, led by Charlie Parker and Dizzy Gillespie. They opened on New York's famous Fifty-second Street, known as "Swing Street" in 1945.

acquired the nickname "Yardbird," or "Bird." They immediately recognized that if Parker was not exactly following in Gillespie's path, he was moving in the same direction. Bird and Diz, as they were now known, teamed up, and together—along with similarly minded musicians like pianist Thelonious Monk, drummer Kenny "Klook" Clarke, and others—began working their various ideas into a musical system. In 1944 and 1945 they began making records using some of these new ideas. In 1945 Parker and Gillespie opened in a small club on New York's famous Fifty-second ("Swing") Street playing the new music, which had acquired the name "bebop," or "bop" as it is now generally known. (The term derives from a phrase Gillespie used to sing to demonstrate some of his ideas.)

Bop was quite different from swing. It used chords and harmonies that were very foreign sounding to most fans of popular music, although they had been used by classical composers for some time. Bop rhythm, too, was quite different from earlier jazz beats—at times it sounded "backward" from the older way of playing. As a consequence, many jazz musicians, critics, and fans set their faces against the new music. Louis Armstrong, a jazz hero for twenty years at that point, called it "modern malice" filled with "weird chords" that did not mean anything.

But on the other hand, a lot of younger musicians and fans, attracted by the fresh sound and the rebellious spirit behind the music, became ardent fans of Parker, Gillespie, and the rest, and very quickly bop moved into the jazz mainstream.

It is generally felt that the genius of the new music, the Louis Armstrong of bop, was Charlie Parker. He was certainly one of the finest improvisers ever in jazz, and his solos on recordings like "Koko," "Parker's Mood," "Just Friends," "Ornithology," and many others are breathtaking, both for the speed at which Parker could play and his unrivaled inventiveness. Gillespie, too, was a great improviser and was responsible for working out much of the theory behind bop. But Parker was the genius, and, for a period, virtually every young saxophonist in jazz was trying to sound like him. Bop would be the basic jazz style for some fifty years.

Another very significant figure in jazz at the time was Thelonious Monk. He was an eccentric character, a big man given to wearing odd hats and a goatee. Sometimes, when he was carried away by the music, he would stand up from the piano bench and dance around the bandstand for a few measures, while the other musicians went on playing.

His piano style, too, was quite unusual. He did not often use the very full stride style, with its powerful bass and busy right hand, nor the high-speed runs of some other very fast bop pianists. His style was spare and "angular," with notes dropped in at surprising places. Thelonious Monk had one of the most individual styles in all of jazz.

Yet another very individual talent to emerge during the bop era was Charlie Mingus. He was a fine bass player, technically very adept and rhythmically very powerful. But he is best known today for his unique compositions. Like Ellington, Mingus composed on the spur of the moment. He would tell his musicians what sort of mood he wanted to create, and leave a good deal of it up to them. Most of his pieces are meant to express moods—"Good-bye Pork Pie Hat" was an elegy on the death of Lester Young, who always wore what was called a porkpie hat in those days. "Better Git It in Your Soul" was meant to recapture the feeling of the church services Mingus attended as a boy.

Bop was not without its rivals for the affection of the public. Coming along at the same time was another movement in modern jazz that at

Charles Mingus began playing in swing bands then switched to bop when it came along in the 1940s. But he is best known for his work from the 1950s, when he showed himself to be one of the most imaginative composers ever in jazz. *Courtesy of CBS.*

the time was known as the "West Coast school," but which is now more accurately known as "cool" jazz. The most important figure in the development of this music was pianist Dave Brubeck. He was interested in classical music as much as in jazz, and studied with the modern composer Darius Milhaud. As early as 1940, when swing was still in its ascendancy, Brubeck was bringing elements of classical music into jazz. He was in the army during World War II, but in 1946 was back in California and in college, studying with Milhaud. With like-minded students he formed the Dave Brubeck Octet. This group, which used a lot of ideas drawn from modern classical music, was too advanced to find much of an audience. Eventually Brubeck formed a quartet, featuring alto saxophonist Paul Desmond. Brubeck was a hard-hitting, busy pianist; Desmond played a very spare line in a light tone. The contrast between their two playing styles worked. Together they would improvise contrapuntal lines that wove back and forth between each other. By the 1950s Brubeck was having a tremendous popular success, particularly among college students, one of the best-known figures in jazz.

The idea of bringing classical music forms into jazz was an obvious one and appealed to many. Back in New York in 1947 and 1948, as bop was taking over, a group of young musicians gathered around arranger Gil Evans, who had written music for various swing bands. This group made a few records built around the ideas of Evans and others. Thinking in a similar way was pianist John Lewis, who in the early 1950s formed one of the most durable of all jazz groups, the Modern Jazz Quartet (MJQ), featuring the hard-swinging bop vibraphonist Milt Jackson. Once again, the music Lewis designed for the MJQ was filled with devices drawn from classical music.

Another important figure in the cool style was trumpeter Miles Davis. The son of a well-to-do dentist, Miles grew up in St. Louis. When young Miles said that he wanted to be a musician, his family insisted that he go to the famous Juilliard School in New York to study classical music. But Davis was far more interested in the new bebop

Perhaps the most popular style of the 1950s, the so-called West Coast, or "cool," school was a more thoughtful and controlled jazz form than the hard-driving bop. The best known of the cool players was the pianist Dave Brubeck, shown here at home with his children, playing a toy guitar for fun. Despite being labeled as a cool player, Brubeck was a strong, powerful pianist. *Courtesy of CBS.*

just coming over the horizon, and he began to skip his classes at Juilliard in order to follow Charlie Parker around from one jazz club to another. Parker took him under his wing, and in time he hired Davis as the trumpeter for his band.

But Davis was not truly a bop musician in his heart. After a time he gravitated to the quieter, more thoughtful cool school. He spent time hanging around with Gil Evans and his group and eventually took over leadership of it. He then took up the modal system, new to jazz at the time, which pared the complex chords of bop down to a very basic level. He quickly became famous for his modal playing. A few years later he hired Gil Evans to write some music for him that owed a lot to classical music. Two of Davis's most famous pieces came out of this collaboration, "Sketches of Spain" and "Porgy and Bess." His work continued to be experimental and spare in the cool manner until, toward the end of his career, he started playing the very thickly textured jazz-rock.

The cool school created a version of jazz that was more recognizable to most audiences, and cool groups like the Brubeck Quartet, the MJQ, and Shorty Rogers and His Giants were very popular playing in this style. But cool nonetheless did not dislodge bop as the main style of jazz.

For a while it appeared that yet another jazz style would do that. In the mid-1950s an alto saxophonist named Ornette Coleman was

One of the most important musical teams of the 1950s and after was the combination of trumpeter Miles Davis and composer and conductor Gil Evans. Davis learned much from Evans as a young musician and later on asked him to work out large scale compositions for him. Two of the most famous pieces turned out by this collaboration are "Sketches of Spain," and a version of "Porgy and Bess," an opera written by George and Ira Gershwin. *Courtesy of CBS.*

Surely the most controversial of all jazz styles was the "free" or "avant-garde" jazz that burst on the scene in the late 1950s with the first recordings by Ornette Coleman. Originally a saxophonist, Coleman later took up the violin and trumpet as well. Despite the great uproar he created with his music at first, Coleman had never been the popular figure that some jazz musicians like Davis, Armstrong, and Coltrane became. Nonetheless, his work continues to be respected by the avant-gardists. *Courtesy of CBS.*

struggling to make a name for himself in Los Angeles. Coleman had played in some rhythm and blues groups, but he wanted to play bop. However, the kind of music that came out of his saxophone was so strange that other musicians would walk off the bandstand when he got up to play. Hurt and discouraged, he nonetheless kept trying and eventually found a group of young players, including Don Cherry, who appreciated what he was trying to do. Almost by chance, a small company recorded the group. The music was so novel, so different, that it caused an immediate jazz sensation. Many musicians, fans, and critics hated it, but it found a lot of supporters, too.

At about the same time, pianist Cecil Taylor was also working on a very experimental new style. This music, too, found more detractors than admirers, but both Taylor and Coleman managed to find a certain amount of work and to record from time to time. Others followed suit. The music was called "free" or "avant-garde" jazz. One of those drawn to it was tenor and soprano saxophonist John Coltrane. He had established himself as a major talent in bop with his work with Miles Davis, but he was reaching for something new, and his pieces like "Ascension" were among the best known of the avant-garde work.

But the avant-garde school did not push bop aside. It was too unstructured to catch a large audience. By the 1960s the real problem for jazz was not its competing styles, but something new—rock. Young people were turning away from the thorny bop and even thornier avant-garde jazz in favor of something simpler. Jazz people grew worried and then despaired as they saw jazz clubs close and recordings dwindle. But Miles Davis went on to introduce yet one more style of jazz.

Through the 1960s Davis was experimenting in a number of directions. He was quite successful for a while. But as the rock boom grew his record sales dwindled. So, in the late 1960s, he began trying a merger of jazz and rock. It was an obvious idea that was being tried by others, but Davis was the one who had the great success with it, with hits like *Bitches Brew* and others that followed. This so-called "fusion" music was not accepted by all jazz people as true jazz; many of them thought that it was basically a form of rock, not a form of jazz.

Dixieland, big band swing, bop, avant-garde, fusion: these are the main stylistic changes that jazz has gone through during its hundred-year history. But we must bear in mind that jazz is a music of individu-

The man who really brought free playing into jazz was John Coltrane. He started as a swing player as a teenager and moved into bop when it came along—his "Giant Steps" is one of the greatest of bop recordings. He took up free jazz after Coleman, Cecil Taylor, and others founded the style, and his "Impressions" became one of the most influential recordings in that style.

als who cannot be easily labeled and put into boxes. Musicians like Armstrong and Goodman started as Dixielanders, but became quintessential swing players; Coltrane played both bop and free jazz; Davis was at home in a number of styles.

Today the most widely played style of jazz is what is called "neo-bop," that is, "new" bop. It is much like the music devised by Parker and Gillespie but permits a certain amount of free jazz playing in the manner of John Coltrane. Among the young jazz musicians working in the neo-bop style are saxophonists Christopher Hollyday and Joshua Redman, trumpeter Roy Hargrove, and pianist Benny Green; but there are many more who are equally interesting.

Miles Davis was a very experimental player, always going off in new directions. Jazz fans were sometimes disappointed with these experiments, especially when he moved into jazz-rock and used electronic instruments in the later years of his life. But his work with Gil Evans, and particularly his 1960s group, including saxophonist Wayne Shorter and drummer Tony Williams, has remained extremely influential up until today. *Courtesy of CBS.*

Despite neo-bop's popularity, the other jazz styles are still very much alive and well. Many Dixieland festivals are held every year: the Sacramento Jazz Jubilee annually features over a hundred Dixieland bands and attracts tens of thousands of listeners. Swing bands are heard regularly, not just in dance halls, but on concert stages like Carnegie Hall. Avant-gardists record and appear from time to time in major jazz clubs. Fusion is still widely popular.

Among the bright new stars in jazz who play the so-called "neo-bop" style are Antonio Hart and Steve Coleman. Most of the young jazz players have studied the music in college and not only have mastered their instruments but have a thorough understanding of music theory. *Courtesy of RCA Records.*

Even though new players with new styles are always coming along, the music of older players stays in fashion. Roy Hargrove is one of the new crop of young stars; Sonny Rollins has been playing jazz for forty years and remains an important innovator. *Courtesy of RCA Records.*

Most young players today are able to move easily from one style to another, so that they can play whatever type of music is called for from one job to the next. It is a very healthy sign that jazz people are finally getting away from the old battles of the styles that so frequently set one group against the next. Today we recognize that there is something of value in all styles of jazz.

CHAPTER 5

THE HEARTBEAT OF JAZZ

Not long ago, archaeologists discovered in a cave in Europe a group of human footprints made thousands of years ago in the clay floor. The clay had subsequently hardened, and the footprints had been preserved for these thousands of years.

Who made these footprints? the archaeologists wanted to know. They studied them and concluded they were made by a single person. From the size and shape they could tell it had been a boy. What was he doing in that cave? He was dancing. What sort of a dance he was doing is not known, but we can easily picture him, dressed in a skirt or short robe of animal fur, possibly wearing some kind of ceremonial headdress, spinning and dancing around and around in that cave in the flickering light of oil lamps. He was a human being, just like us; and just like us, he liked to dance.

All peoples dance. Some dance in religious ceremonies for marriages and funerals, some dance to celebrate a victory in battle or a successful hunt, some—like us—dance mainly for fun. But dancing is one of the great bonds that join humans into one big family.

During the 1920s one of Chicago's most famous dance places was the Midway Gardens, where a lot of top jazz musicians, including the teenage Benny Goodman, played. Midway Gardens was designed by the famous American architect Frank Lloyd Wright.

And dancing is rhythmic. To be sure, there are a few forms of dancing that are not done to a steady beat: some kinds of ballet, especially modern ballet, are not always rhythmic. But at bottom, one of the main functions of dancing is to express rhythm. We like the feeling of our arms, legs, torsos moving to a steady beat. There is something exhilarating about it.

Why should rhythmic movement seem to mean a lot to human beings of all different races and nationalities? This is a matter that psychologists are studying but they have not come to any firm conclusions. It is clear, however, that rhythm is a regular part of human life. We walk and run to a regular beat—imagine trying to walk with one leg going to one beat, the other leg going to a different one. Our hearts pump to a steady beat, although the tempo speeds up and slows down depending on how active we are. The same is true of our breathing.

But interestingly enough, we do a lot of things to rhythm that do not really have to be done to a steady beat. For example, when you stir something, like a cake mix in a bowl, or sugar in a cup of coffee, we generally do it to a steady beat. We do not have to do it this way, but it just seems more natural. Rhythm is a very basic element in human life.

It is therefore not surprising that it is basic to music and dance. These two human activities are very much bound together. We almost always dance to music, and a great deal of music was created specifically for dancing.

This is certainly true of jazz and its forebears. The music of the Africans who were brought to the Americas as slaves was highly rhythmic. As stated earlier, it was built around polyrhythms. One person who heard a black boatsman singing in time with the motion of the oars wrote:

> One noticeable thing about their boat-songs was that they seemed often to be sung just a trifle behind time; in "Rainfall," for instance, "Believer cry holy" would seem to occupy more than its share of the stroke, the "holy" being prolonged until the very next stroke; indeed, I think Jerry often hung on his oar a little just there before dipping it in again (cited in James Lincoln Collier, *The Making of Jazz* [New York, Dell Publishing, 1978]).

It appears that these black slaves were loosening their melody lines from the beat, to give the effect of two beats, or meters, being played simultaneously.

But of course they could not produce this effect unless there was a beat there to begin with. And here lies one of the major differences between black-based music like jazz and ordinary "Western" music, as the music that grew out of Europe is frequently called. Western music—like symphonies, folk tunes, marches, "Happy Birthday," "The Star-Spangled Banner"—is written so that it is possible to feel its beat; we have little trouble tapping our foot to the beat of a march or to "Happy Birthday."

But when a musician is deliberately cutting the melody loose from the beat, and putting notes in "wrong" places, it is hard to tap your foot to it. In order to make it clear where the beat was, the musicians always had a ground beat present. This ground beat could be provided by drums or some other musical instrument but with blacks of the nineteenth century, it was more often made in other ways. It might be the sound of dancers' feet pounding on a dance-hall floor, the ring of a sledgehammer on a railroad spike as workers sang a song to relieve the tedium of labor, or by the hand claps of worshipers in a church.

A jazz band almost always has a rhythm section laying down a steady beat, against which the other musicians play melodies that are slightly off beat in various ways. These rhythmic departures from strict time can be quite obvious, but more often they are subtle and almost impossible to grasp by ear alone. However, in recent years, cognitive psychologists, using modern digital equipment, have examined jazz rhythms in fine detail, and there is no question that jazz musicians habitually place their notes slightly away from the beat. Sometimes they strike a note about halfway between two beats, but more often it is a matter of hitting the note just a little bit early or a little bit late. The difference may be as small as a twentieth of a second, but even though we cannot actually pinpoint a difference this small, it is enough to provide, at least in part, the swing that is so important to jazz.

But there is a second, related thing that jazz musicians do to their music to punch up the rhythm. In any kind of music, we do not play just one note to a beat, marching along one after another. In Western music, some notes are given a beat and a half, some two beats, sometimes five or ten beats. But beats are also divided, with two, three, four, or more notes per beat. The most common divisions of the beat in Western music are into two equal parts (eighth notes), three equal parts (triplets or six-eight time), four parts (sixteenth notes), and unequal divisions like two to one (tied triplets) and three to one (dotted eighth and sixteenth notes).

In jazz, players divide beats irregularly according to their own feeling for how they like to swing their music. Some players, like the great saxophonist Coleman Hawkins, divide their beats very unevenly; others, like Dizzy Gillespie, divide them more evenly. But always in jazz the first of each pair of notes is emphasized at the expense of the second.

This playing around with the beat—stretching out notes beyond their expected length, jumping them in early or holding them back late, splitting them up unevenly, at times playing whole patches of melody that have little to do with the beat at all—all of this is at the essence of jazz, its rhythmic heart.

But of course it can only work if there is a ground beat being hammered out by something or somebody. As I have said, rhythm can be

The Original Dixieland Jazz Band used just drums and piano in its rhythm section. Early jazz was often presented in vaudeville as a comedy act. Here the musicians are trying to strike humorous poses.

provided by dancers' feet or the ring of a hammer. The same is true of jazz: rhythm can be provided just by a piano player's left hand, by somebody beating with his hands on a tabletop. But more often a jazz band has some sort of formal rhythm section, made up of a combination of drums, piano, string bass or tuba, guitar or banjo, and, at times, a low instrument like a bass saxophone.

The early New Orleans jazz bands often used rhythm sections of guitar, string bass, drums and, at times, piano. Of course it was difficult to march with a string bass, and guitars were too soft to be heard outside, so for parades rhythm was provided by tubas and drums, with one drummer playing the bass and clanging a cymbal attached to its top, while another drummer played the snare.

Rhythm sections came in all shapes and sizes in these early jazz bands, sometimes using two guitars, sometimes only bass and guitar. Many of the famous Louis Armstrong Hot Five records had only banjo and piano, and the Original Dixieland Jazz Band, the first to become nationally famous, used piano and drums.

But by the early 1920s, rhythm sections had settled down to piano, drums, tuba, and banjo. Moreover, the drum set, originally a snare drum played with sticks and a bass drum struck by means of a foot pedal, grew more and more grandiose. Tom-toms, which produced a hollow sound, became standard. Cymbals of various sizes and sounds were added. Sizzle cymbals had little rivets set loosely in holes around the rim that made a "sissing" sound as they rattled. Other devices, like temple blocks, which made a hollow tap, and cowbells, which produced a flat ring, were added. Most significantly, by the late 1920s the hi-hat, a device made up of two cymbals that could be opened and closed by means of a foot pedal, had come into existence. The hi-hat cymbals could be clashed together and would make different sounds when struck if they were opened or closed.

In the early jazz bands, drummers mainly kept time on the snare drums, frequently using a *boom-dada, boom-dada* pattern. Pianists thumped out chords or used the stride oompah bass. Basses or tubas

The bass is a very important instrument in the rhythm section because it provides not only a percussive beat like a drum but can outline the chords to support soloists. It is very rare to see two bass players in one band but it happened once when Duke Ellington wanted to bring in the brilliant young bassist Jimmy Blanton (left) but did not want to fire his old bassist, Billy Taylor.

played only every other beat. The total effect was a sort of two-four, rocking-back-and-forth feel, which was an essential element of the swing of these early bands.

By the early 1930s, rhythm sections were seeking an easier, more flowing rhythm. The somewhat clunky banjos were replaced by guitars, tubas by string basses for a lighter, more precise sound. Drummers began keeping time mainly on the hi-hat in a sort of *ching, chika-ching* pattern, which was also lighter in sound. Basses played on all beats. The back-and-forth rocking swing of the early jazz bands now gave way to a steady, flowing beat.

With the arrival of dissonant harmonies of modern jazz in the late 1940s, the main beat was moved from the hi-hat to the so-called "top cymbal," a big cymbal set on top of the bass drum, which was played with a swishing sound that, at fast tempos, seemed to blend into one blur. Bass drums were used only occasionally for accents.

The musician responsible for making some of these changes was drummer Kenny Clarke. He had been working in Teddy Hill's swing

The drums have always been at the heart of jazz. Some jazz bands have worked without drums, but they are rare. The first jazz bands in New Orleans usually had only a snare and a bass drum. But soon after drum sets began to swell. Today they usually include a snare, bass drum, small and large tom-toms, and several cymbals. A key part of the drum set is the hi-hat, two cymbals rigged so they can be clashed by means of a foot pedal. Here Duke Ellington is talking to his longtime drummer, Sonny Greer. His set includes tympany, shells, and gongs. Much of this equipment was for show—Greer did not play the tympany and rarely used gongs.

band, which played a lot of fast, hot numbers the dancers liked. Clarke said, "We played so many flag-wavers, man, you know, fast up-tempo numbers like 'The Harlem Twister', that my right foot got paralyzed—so I cut it all out except now and then" (cited in Collier, *The Making of Jazz*, 347). That is to say, he used his right foot on the bass drum pedal only to occasionally "drop bombs," as the saying went, and kept the beat going on the top cymbal. He said later:

> In 1937 I'd got tired of playing like Jo Jones. It was time for jazz drummers to move ahead. I took the main beat away from the bass drum and up to the top cymbal. I found out I could get pitch and timbre variations up there, according to the way the stick struck the cymbal, and a pretty sound. The beat had a better flow. It was lighter

and tastier. That left me free to use the bass drum, the tom-toms and snare for accents [cited in Collier, *The Making of Jazz*, 347–48].

Pianists, too, began to accent sparingly to stay out of the way of the complex harmonies played by the horns, and guitars were dropped altogether for the same reason. Frequently drummers clashed the hi-hat on the second and fourth beats of each measure for an offbeat effect. Now, the main timekeeper, supplying the basic beat, was the string bass.

This rhythm section of bass, drums, and piano, with the bassist as the timekeeper, has become the mainstay in jazz.

One of the key points about jazz is that the rhythm section is supposed to keep perfect time: How can horn players drop in notes just fractionally off the beat if they cannot be sure of where the beat is? Jazz rhythm players pride themselves on being able to keep perfect time. Or so it was believed until very recently.

New studies done by cognitive psychologists using modern equipment have shown that while jazz bands do keep very good time, it is not perfect: some beats are played imperceptibly longer than others. Furthermore, there is a tendency for bands to speed up and slow down fractionally at times, perhaps when a certain soloist comes in, or when a chorus is ended and a new one begins. These shifts in tempo are subtle, in most cases imperceptible, even to the musicians themselves. These are, however, a regular part of jazz. Some jazz musicians have always been aware of this. The famous drummer Gene Krupa once said that he did not believe in keeping perfect time. Apparently a good many other musicians agreed with him, for he played with many of the greatest: Benny Goodman, who Krupa worked with off and on all his life, said that Krupa was his favorite drummer.

In jazz, tempo is a fluid, living thing. That is why the music never seems quite as lively and exciting when a drum machine is supplying the ground beat. You cannot swing with a machine; only human beings can do that.

CHAPTER 6

MAKING IT UP AS YOU GO ALONG

One thing that puzzles people about jazz is improvisation: How is a player able to create a whole stream of music, minute after minute, in what often seems like an effortless fashion? How can a player, night after night, produce all that wonderful music with—so it seems—nothing to guide him or her but *inspiration*, whatever that curious term means?

Improvising a jazz solo is at once easier, and harder, than it seems. On the one hand, even a beginning musician can learn certain fairly simple rules of harmony and melody that will provide him or her with musical ideas to work from. That is to say, if you learn that the harmony at a certain place in a tune is based on an F major chord, you know that you can play around with the notes that make up that chord—F, A, C—putting them together in any order and fashion that suits you. You will then be improvising.

On the other hand, improvising something exciting and distinctive, the kind of thing that sends shivers up listeners' spines, is something

Roy Eldridge was a short but powerful player, and he was nicknamed "Little Jazz" by his fellow musicians. Jazz musicians tend to be quite critical of themselves, always wishing they had done something different in a particular solo. Eldridge was rarely completely satisfied with his own playing. *Courtesy of CBS.*

that even the best improvisers are not able to do all the time. Once, trumpeter Roy Eldridge and saxophonist Coleman Hawkins, two of the finest of all jazz musicians, were talking with some fans during a break at the club where they were playing. One of the fans asked Eldridge how often he played a solo that truly satisfied him. He thought about it for a minute and said, "Once a month, maybe." Then the fan asked Hawkins the same question. "Once a year, if I'm lucky," he said.

Of course these musicians were being unduly hard on themselves. They probably played a fine solo at least once a night, and many times, when they were "on," played brilliantly *all* night. But they had a point: it simply is not given to human beings to be endlessly creative minute after minute. Just as a pitcher will be unhittable one time, and unable to get anyone out the next time, so jazz musicians have their good days and bad. Sometimes it all comes flowing out effortlessly; sometimes the fingers feel stiff and clumsy, the mind dull, unable to come up with anything interesting. The much-admired early New Orleanian clarinetist Leon Ropollo was said to have thrown his clarinet in Lake Pontchartrain outside the city one night when he could not catch hold of something that was echoing in his head.

According to one dictionary, to improvise means "to perform or provide without previous preparation." This may be a good definition for some kinds of things, but it is certainly not true of jazz. The improvising jazz musician is thoroughly prepared before he steps onto the bandstand. We might make a comparison with sports. A shortstop fielding a ground ball is improvising, in the sense that no two grounders will come at him—or her—in exactly the same way. Moreover, the circumstances will always be different. Is there a runner on third base? If so, will he try to score on the play? Is the field wet or dry? Is his team ahead or behind and by how much? How many outs are there? Is it early or late in the game? These, and other factors, help to determine what the shortstop must do. Baseball players are continually thinking about these things as the game progresses, and planning what they will do in various circumstances.

The shortstop is thoroughly prepared before the ball is hit. He has fielded thousands of ground balls before, many times with runners on third, in wet and dry conditions, early and late in games, with his team ahead and behind. He has a pretty good idea of what to expect over the next three or four seconds, and to a considerable extent he can put himself on automatic pilot and let his reflexes take over. Indeed, he has to: there is no way to plan out how to field a grounder. You have to let your hands, arms, and legs do what you have spent many hours training them to do.

We all do a great deal of improvising during the course of our lives. When you hop on your bicycle to ride over to visit a friend, you do not plan out exactly what you are going to do through the course of the ride. Instead, you "improvise" according to circumstances—stop for a red light, go through if it is green, skirt around a puddle in the road, slow down when a car makes a turn in front of you. But you are

Jack Teagarden was one of the finest of all jazz trombonists. With much practice when he was a boy, he developed a way of playing the trombone that was quite different from the early New Orleans style, in which trombonists played a lot of slurs and low notes. Teagarden mainly played in the upper register, and he used a lot of lip slurs, which sound easy but are quite difficult to perform.

well prepared: you know how to ride a bike, understand what red and green lights mean, have learned the hard way what happens when you splash through a puddle.

It is the same when you are standing around at the bus stop talking with some friends. You have not come there with a prepared speech. Instead, you "improvise" your conversation as you go along, responding to what others are saying, adding things that happen to pop into your head, and so forth. But once again, you are prepared: you under-

JAZZ: AN AMERICAN SAGA

stand English, know the foibles of the teacher the gossip is about, are familiar with the hot musical groups the talk turns to.

So it is with improvising jazz musicians: they are thoroughly prepared before they are on the bandstand. They have spent countless hours learning how to play their instruments. Readers who study music know how much time goes into developing the skills needed to play a drum, a trombone, a piano. Serious music students at conservatories think nothing of practicing eight hours a day, besides studying music theory, music history, and related subjects. Even players with long experience practice at least a couple of hours a day just to keep their "chops" up. Concert pianists may practice all day long for weeks to prepare a new piece for a concert.

Just like the athlete, musicians must train their reflexes so that their arms, fingers, and lips respond properly without them having to think about it. Dizzy Gillespie remembered that when he was a teenager at the Laurinburg Institute in North Carolina, "I practiced constantly, until all times of the night, anytime I wanted. I'd practice the trumpet and then the piano for twenty-four hours straight if they didn't come around and shut me up when they checked the locks every night" (Dizzy Gillespie with Al Fraser, *To Be or Not to Bop* [New York: Doubleday, 1979], 38). A story that is told about Art Tatum, one of the most admired pianists in jazz, is how he used to practice his mistakes: if he played a wrong note in a fast run—which he rarely did—he would already have worked out something to play that would make the wrong note sound right. He also carried around with him a pair of walnuts that he would constantly squeeze together to keep up the strength in his hands. The walnuts were worn round as golf balls. Benny Goodman, long after he had become one of the greatest of all jazz clarinetists, continued to practice every day. In fact, he was practicing the day he died.

The improvising musician is first of all a well-trained instrumentalist. This was not always the case. Many of the early jazz players, like those kids in that sunlit barn struggling to play their new music, were poorly trained. As a teenager, Louis Armstrong received some instruction, but for the most part he was self-taught. Unfortunately, he picked up the bad habit of pressing the trumpet too hard against his lips on the high notes, and over the years did considerable damage to them. Some of the early jazz musicians played out of tune and really did not execute very well. Certain jazz critics concluded from this that a jazz musician could make more honest music if he was not technically proficient on his instrument. In the 1940s some jazz writers discovered down in New Orleans several of the original jazz pioneers, who had been passed by and who had had to work at day labor on farms to survive. The writers were terribly excited to find people who they thought could re-create jazz as it had originally sounded, and they made recordings of the old musicians. While the music certainly did have a rough power, most other musicians laughed at it for being out of tune and not well played. The point is that these old musicians did not intend to play out of tune; it was that they had been out of practice for so long they could not do better.

Today no jazz musician can have much success unless he or she is thoroughly trained. And this means not only having the ability to play an instrument skillfully: it also means knowing music theory thoroughly.

Music theory is a subject that sometimes scares off young performers. It should not. It is no harder to learn than arithmetic or spelling. It is just a matter of study and practice. Anyone interested can certainly find books that will introduce them to the subject. Music theory tells you what notes go along with other notes—that is to say, how to group notes to make up chords and melodies. Jazz musicians know music theory so well that it is almost instinctive. It gives them something to fall back on; as in the example I used earlier, where the soloist knows that when there is an F major chord in the harmony, he can play the notes F, A, and C in any order and combination he wants.

But for the most part, jazz soloists are not thinking about music theory when they are playing. Instead, they are listening to what is going on around them, absorbing it all, and playing something that comes into their heads in response. There is a famous story concerning Charlie Parker and the invention of his style, which led the way to bop. Parker was playing at a chili place with a little group. He later recalled, "I'd been getting bored with the stereotyped [chord] changes that were being used all the time at the time, and I kept thinking there's bound to be something else. I could hear it sometimes, but I couldn't play it. Well, that night I was working over 'Cherokee,' and as I did I found that by using the higher intervals of a chord . . . I could play the thing I'd been hearing" (Shapiro and Hentoff, *Hear Me Talkin' to Ya*, 354).

The jazz pioneers were often self-taught, fairly rough players who worked out their methods from doing. Today jazz players must understand music theory thoroughly. Gerry Mulligan, shown here, was not only a fine baritone saxophone soloist, but had studied theory carefully and was known as much for his arranging as for his playing. *Courtesy of CBS.*

It is not necessary to understand the technical point to get the idea. Parker had been sensing that there was something else he could play against the harmonies of "Cherokee," but it kept eluding him—he could not quite get his hands on it because it was something revolutionary in musical terms. But that particular night it burst into his mind and he understood what it was.

Jazz musicians must have good "ears." They must recognize what they are hearing, and be able to play it back. If the piano player moves from an F major chord to a Bb minor chord, the soloist should be able to recognize what is happening and improvise something that fits. And if he hears in his head a piece of melody, he must be able to play it on his instrument without having to think about it.

To the beginner this may sound very difficult, even miraculous, but it is only a matter of study and practice. It is probably true that some

A rare photograph of three of the finest of the swing tenor saxophonists: Coleman Hawkins, Lester Young, and Ben Webster. Hawkins was a master of theory and played a driving, complex style, using many variations on chord changes. By contrast, Lester Young played a light, airy style, using the simplest of harmonies. Webster began by imitating Hawkins but then developed a simpler, more breathy style that was particularly suited to ballads. Each of them found his own individual voice and can be instantly identified by knowledgeable jazz fans. *Courtesy of CBS.*

people are naturally more gifted than others in respect to their ears; nonetheless, anyone who wants to develop an ear sufficient for improvising a jazz solo can do so through training.

This, then, is the essence of the improvising process: musical ideas pop into your head, and because you are well-trained on your instrument, you are able to play them instantly. Where do those musical ideas come from? A lot of places. They may be suggested by something somebody else has just played, or is playing. They may come from a bit of melody you heard on the radio the day before that stuck in your mind. It may simply come out of thin air.

Certainly feelings have a lot to do with it. How a jazz musician plays at any given moment depends a great deal on his mood—whether he had a fight with his boss, got a good review for a record, or has a cold. Duke Ellington, one of the greatest of all jazz composers, would deliberately court a mood when he was working on a piece. Of one of his blue pieces, he said that it was "just a story about a little girl and a little boy. They are about eight and the girl loves the boy. They never speak of it, of course, but she just likes the way he wears his hat. Every day he comes to her house at a certain time and she sits in her window and waits. Then one day he doesn't come" (James Lincoln Collier, *Duke Ellington* [New York: Oxford University Press, 1987], 151). The tune tells how she feels. Another of his compositions, called "Happy Go Lucky Local," is about the fireman on a little local train who blows the train whistle as he passes the houses of his girlfriends. Ellington would tell his star trumpeter Cootie Williams, who was noted for his growl style, to sound like "a hungry little lion cub that wants his dinner but can't find his mother" (Collier, *Duke Ellington*).

Ellington would also draw on things he saw as he traveled with his band around the country. Coming into Pittsburgh in those days the night sky would be full of flames from the chimneys of the steel mills; Ellington wrote a tune to capture the feeling of the sky flashing with fire. Another of his most famous pieces, "Harlem Airshaft," is about the sounds and smells that floated around in an apartment building airshaft—people quarreling, the smell of turkey roasting, two neighbors gossiping. "Harlem Airshaft" uses a real mix of melodies to suggest this confusion.

Feelings and memories of things past are important to jazz musicians. But nobody can count on having the right sort of feelings all the time. What if no musical ideas pop into your head when you are playing a solo? In truth, that is a very common experience, even for many of the finest jazz soloists. Therefore, most jazz musicians have worked out for themselves things to play when they draw a blank. For one, they often fall back on their knowledge of musical theory, which tells them that on this F major chord they can play around with F, A, C, and on the Bb minor chord following, they can use a Bb, Db, and F, among other notes.

For another, they can return to the melody of the song they are playing. Louis Armstrong was notable for using the melody of the tune in his improvising. He might play a bit of the melody straight, follow that with something suggested by the melody but different from it, return to the melody briefly, then play something freely improvised before approaching the melody again. Indeed, in some of his performances he improvised very little: his well-known solo on "Jubilee" is little more than the melody played straight.

Jazz musicians are not inclined to talk about these things a lot, for it might sound boastful; but they think about their improvising methods a good deal more than they admit. What should I be doing that I'm not doing? How can I approach fast tunes so as not to get myself tangled up? Take the case of Armstrong once again: in his early years he was a very "busy" player, cramming in notes and ideas as fast as they spilled out of his fertile mind. At that time, when he was still unknown to the general public, although already much admired by musicians, he was not working constantly. He might have a week, or even several weeks, off here and there. Furthermore, he was usually not the only soloist in the groups he played in, just one of several.

But then, around 1930, Armstrong started to move into stardom. Now the public wanted as much of him as it could get. Armstrong

Pee Wee Russell (left) developed a highly individual style filled with biting twists and bends. Jimmy Guiffre (right) was an entirely different sort of player, very well trained in modern theory and possessor of a smooth style. Yet the two of them made a fascinating duet called "The River." Fine jazz musicians find ways to work together no matter how different their styles. *Courtesy of CBS.*

wanted to work as much as possible, and his managers kept him working, 365 days a year. He was now carrying the whole band himself. On virtually every tune he would play the opening melody, sing a chorus, play an improvised trumpet solo of one or more choruses, and finish with a flourish on a high note. It was a tremendously demanding schedule, particularly for a man with lip problems. As a consequence, he changed from the very busy style of his earlier years to a much sparer style, where he played many fewer notes, leaving many more open spaces in his improvised melody than he had done before. Compare his 1927 version of "Struttin' with Some Barbecue" with the 1936 version. Armstrong plays 50 percent more notes in the early version than in the later one. There is more open space in the second version, too: only six beats of rest in the first version (out of 128 beats) but as many as twenty-eight beats of rest in the second, leaving more than 20 percent of the solo open. Clearly, Armstrong has given some thought to his playing methods.

Finally, jazz improvisers get a lot of their musical ideas from themselves, from what they have just played. Let us suppose you come up

MAKING IT UP AS YOU GO ALONG

with a little three-note figure. You might then play it several times going down, several times going up, going up and down. You might turn it upside down or play it backward, you might simply repeat it, you might play several variations on it.

I do not mean that jazz soloists think such things through in the course of playing. They do not possibly have the time to do that. But they probably will have developed a habit of using certain of these devices in their playing. Many of the early Dixieland clarinet players, like Larry Shields, Johnny Dodds, and Frank Teschemacher, habitually played "saw-toothed" figures in which a little two-note idea was repeated downward step by step. Lester Young liked to hammer away at a note repeatedly, sometimes playing it with different fingering to give every other note a slightly different sound. Habit, unquestionably, is important to jazz improvisers, and those habits of playing often become the trademarks by which we recognize them.

Only the greatest of jazz improvisers have a steady flow of fresh ideas. It was said that Charlie Parker could think so far ahead that he could change what he was going to play several times before he got there. But even Parker had his habits—he plays the "bridge" portion on his masterpiece "Koko" more or less the same both times through.

Fortunately for those of us who are not blessed with the flow of ideas of a Charlie Parker or a John Coltrane, making up new melodies is not what jazz is all about. Indeed, it is not the most important thing. Jazz is not so much about *which* notes are played but *how* those notes are played. The most brilliant musical ideas do not mean much in jazz if they are played exactly straight. They must be made to swing, must be inflected, or tinted, in various ways, to give them life and meaning. Some very fine jazz players, like the Dixielander "Wild Bill" Davison and the bebopper Sonny Stitt, used the same stock of ideas over and over for a good portion of their solos. Armstrong, as we have seen, was a great player of the melody of songs he liked, but he was not alone: many great jazz improvisers, like Benny Goodman and Charlie Parker, often played songs more or less as written. The first records Goodman made with his celebrated trio, such as "Body and Soul," contained a great deal of unadorned melody, and Charlie Parker recorded a whole album of tunes by the famous songwriter Cole Porter in which he played a lot of Porter's melodies straight. It was how they inflected, or colored, the melodies that counted.

We have looked at some of the ways notes can be inflected in the chapter on rhythm. You can play notes a little early or a little late. You can swoop up to them or curl down from them. You can play them louder or softer. You can add vibrato (that is, a fast quaver) at various parts of a note. You can "bend" them, that is, let them rise or fall slightly as they go along. You can change their sounds from note to note, or even during one note. Trumpeters and trombonists in particular use a lot of different kinds of mutes to change the sound of their notes. One of the best known of these is the so-called "plunger" mute, which is used to open and close the bell of the horn, producing a dras-

No jazz musician can think up fresh musical ideas solo after solo, night after night. Very often *how* you play is more important than *what* you play; playing with a lot of swing and emotion is what counts the most. "Wild Bill" Davison was not nearly as inventive as the great Louis Armstrong, whom he vastly admired, but was nonetheless a driving, fiery player who was always exciting to listen to. *Courtesy of CBS.*

Guitarist Eddie Condon (center) refused to take solos and was better known for organizing record dates and running his jazz club than for his playing. But he was a very good rhythm guitarist whom other musicians liked to play with for his swing. In the end that is what jazz is all about. *Courtesy of CBS.*

tic change in sound. But it is also possible to add growls to the sound through the use of "throat tones," a sort of rasping in the throat. Bubber Miley, Duke Ellington's first trumpet star, was a master at combining the plunger mute with throat tones. His dramatic growling on early Ellington pieces like "Black and Tan Fantasy" and "East St. Louis Toodle-Oh" was important in making the Ellington orchestra a hit.

How do you know when to growl, when to play a note late, when to play it early? That is a question I cannot answer. These fine details of jazz playing cannot be planned. They have to simply come out of you at the moment. You do not control them, they *happen* to you. It is a little as if the music is playing you, rather than you playing the music.

Nor is this the sort of thing you can learn to do through formal study. Aspiring jazz musicians must listen to a lot of jazz, must play it as often as they can. In time, these things will come of their own accord. And when they do, the music becomes your own, for it is these little personal touches that give jazz the individual sound that lets the personality of the player shine through the music.

SELECTED DISCOGRAPHY

There exist in libraries and archives thousands of jazz recordings in the form of 78s, LPs, tape cassettes, and CDs. It would be the work of years for students to sample even a small amount of this music. The sensible thing for anyone interested in exploring this music is to start with a few of the most important works and then to listen more carefully to the performers or types of jazz that most interest him or her.

The following is a very brief list of the critically important recordings that anyone interested in jazz will know about.

The Louis Armstrong Hot Five and Hot Seven. All of this series offers rewards. The best-known songs are "West End Blues," "Muggles," and "Tight Like This."

Bix Beiderbecke. Bix recorded with various combinations. His key recordings are "I'm Coming Virginia" and "Singing the Blues."

Jelly Roll Morton. Morton made many important piano recordings, including "The Pearls" and "King Porter Stomp," but he is best known for his Red Hot Peppers records like "The Chant" and "Sidewalk Blues."

Duke Ellington. The Ellington Orchestra lasted for almost fifty years and covered many styles. The early records that made his name are "Black and Tan Fantasy" and "East St. Louis Toodle-Oh." Among his masterpieces from the later period are "Main Stem," "Harlem Airshaft," and "Ko-Ko."

Benny Goodman. Goodman started the swing-band craze. His classics include "Don't Be That Way" and "King Porter Stomp." Also important are his small-group records like "Air Mail Special" and "Dinah."

Lester Young. One of the most influential saxophonists in jazz, Young worked for several years with Count Basie, with whom he made classic solos like "One O'Clock Jump." A lot of his best work is with small groups, as on such recordings as "Lady Be Good," and "Shoe Shine Swing."

Charlie Parker. Among his best-known solos are "Now's the Time," "Billie's Bounce," and especially the high-tempo "Koko."

Dizzy Gillespie. Gillespie had a big band for a brief time with which he made records like "Cubana Be" and "Manteca," but he is best known for his small-group recordings, such as "Groovin' High" and "Salt Peanuts."

Billie Holiday. Widely acknowledged as one of the greatest of all jazz singers, Billie's best recordings were her early ones, like "I Wished On the Moon," and "What a Little Moonlight Can Do."

Art Tatum. The master technician of jazz, Tatum made hundreds of solo recordings. He especially liked playing "Willow, Weep for Me" and very fast tunes like "Get Happy."

Miles Davis. Davis kept changing styles over time, but his best-known works are the big band suites arranged by Gil Evans, such as "Porgy and Bess," and "Sketches of Spain," and pieces like "All Blues" from the famous *Kind of Blue* album.

John Coltrane. Like other great jazz musicians, Coltrane began in one school (bebop) and moved into another (free jazz). His classic bop recording is "Giant Steps." His best-known later works are *A Love Supreme* and "My Favorite Things."

Ornette Coleman. Coleman is the best known of the avant-garde musicians. Among his records that startled the jazz world are pieces like "Lonely Woman" and "Congeniality."

The foregoing list leaves out many great jazz musicians like Sonny Rollins, Thelonious Monk, Jack Teagarden, and others. However, if you look back into the text, you will see that I list key compositions as I discuss each artist. The book's index can lead you to just about any kind of jazz you like.

INDEX

(Page numbers in *italic* refer to illustrations.)

781.65   Collier, James
COL   Lincoln, 1928-

         Jazz.

$18.00   200216